NEW YORK DIARY
Peter Bialobrzeski

March 29 – April 8, 2023

Hartmann books

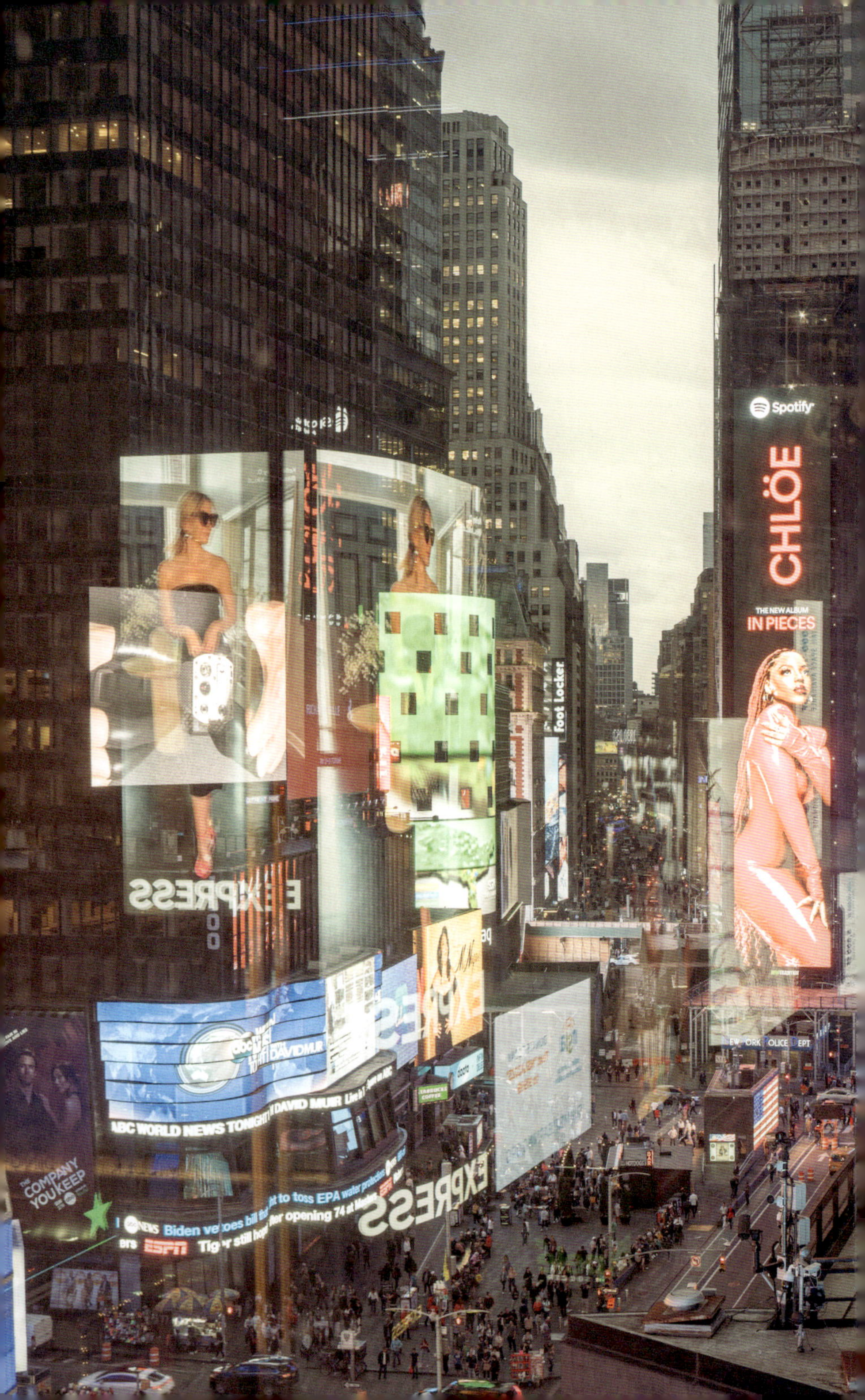
Spotify
CHLÖE
THE NEW ALBUM
IN PIECES
foot Locker
ABC WORLD NEWS TONIGHT
DAVID MUIR
THE COMPANY YOU KEEP
ESPN

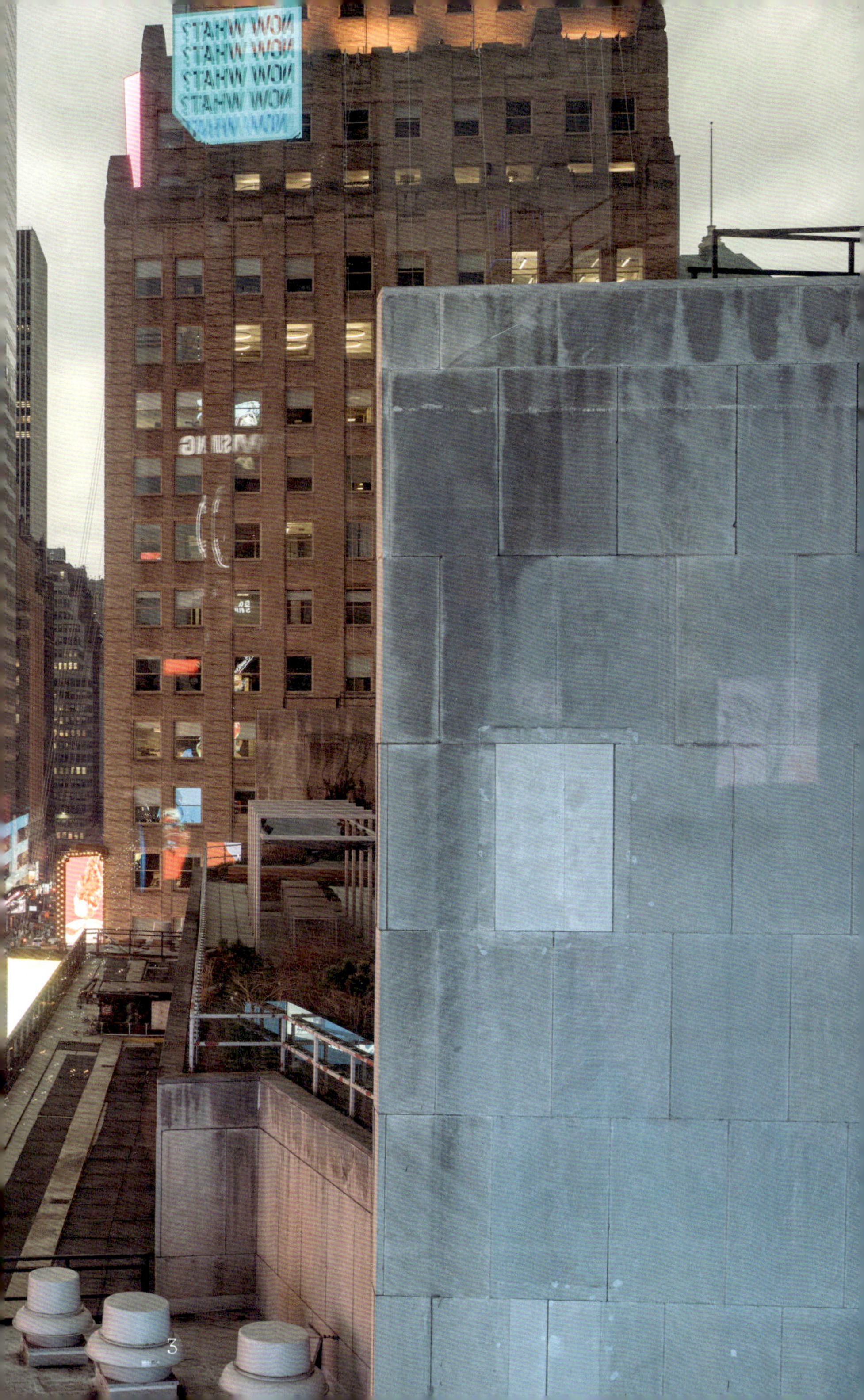

NEW YORK DIARY
Peter Bialobrzeski

→March 29, 2023 It is shortly before six a.m. when I board the express subway to Brooklyn. My fellow passengers, commuters from the Bronx heading to Manhattan, seem as tired as I am. Most of them seem to be service workers; the first lighter-skinned person joins the car at Eighty-Sixth Street. On the way back, the situation is similar: no white faces north of Central Park. From the local news section of the *New York Times*, I learn that Representative Jaamal Bowman, a Democrat from the Bronx, has come to TikTok's defense. He has 159,000 followers and says it is a "great way to communicate with young voters and activists." The paper admits that his videos are actually pretty funny.
→March 30, 2023 Visitors to New York must be prepared to encounter a lot of clichés. Times Square has always been one of them. My last visit to New York was in 2008. Now I am overwhelmed, almost shocked, by the sheer number of LED screens screaming advertisements at the thousands of tourists posing for selfies in front of them. I begin to get a headache and go home to the Bronx.
→March 31, 2023 Meanwhile, in another part of the city, a grand jury has voted to indict Donald Trump, according to his lawyer, who revealed that the former president will face thirty-four counts when he's arraigned next week. According to the *New York Post*, the indicted former president made the wires of his *Truth Social* network glow by accusing political enemies of this and that.
→April 1, 2023 Dinner last night at the *National Arts Club* at the invitation of a friend and long-time New York art dealer. It was a memorable evening with pleasant people, nice conversations, and a funny hat party in the next room. The lavish, exclusive soiree ends for me on the 4 subway train heading north. A family of three gets on the train. The man asks if anyone could spare some toiletries for his wife, as the family is temporarily homeless. People start handing him soda cans, snacks, and other small items. I have just had a wonderful meal in a wonderful setting, and I wonder—not for the first time—who is actually throwing the dice. →April 2, 2023 Porn star *Stormy Daniels* on Twitter: "Thank you all for your support and love! I have so many messages coming in that I can't respond ... also don't want to spill my champagne." For those who don't remember, she's the one who started the lawsuit against Donald Trump. The champagne, according to the *New York Post*, was uncorked to celebrate incoming orders for her personal merchandise, #teamstormy T-shirts, and autographed

posters of herself in sexy lingerie.
→April 3, 2023 The *New York Post* devotes most of its venom these days to accusing Trump's political opponents of treason. Moreover, according to the same news organ, it highlights that the corpse flower has begun to bloom in the Bronx Botanical Gardens for the first time in four years. It takes its name from the fact that its smell resembles that of a decomposing body. For an odorless experience, you can watch a real-time video online. Meanwhile, the *New York Times* reports that Trump's team believes this indictment will help him raise money and could give him a boost. Unbelievable but true: under the American Constitution, it would be possible for him to govern from prison.
→April 4, 2023 "What are you filming?" asks a young professional. When I explain what I'm doing, she invites me to take pictures from a terrace of the hotel where she works. This would not happen back home in Hamburg, a young woman talking to a middle-aged man on the street. Meanwhile, just a few blocks downtown, former President Trump is turning himself in before his arraignment. Several live blogs are reporting that the defendant has arrived in an eleven-car motorcade outside the District Attorney's office in Lower Manhattan.
→April 5, 2023 Although the Bronx is not my photographic subject, it is where I am staying. According to Mike, my host, the Bronx is the inner-city neighborhood with the lowest median income in the country. →April 6, 2023 In Manhattan, an "architectural gem" goes on the market for twenty-eight million dollars, while in the absence of news on Donald, the *Daily Mail* reports that Melania Trump is fed up with her husband's affairs but will never file for divorce. If that weren't enough: actress Jessica Chastain's outfit is commented on as she grabs a coffee in Midtown. Male plastic surgery is also on the rise, but men are being secretive about it. Such a pleasure to be leafing through the tabloids!
→April 8, 2023 A visit to the *Museum of Modern Art* turns out to be a disappointment. The way the staff handles the crowds reminds me of an airport. This feeling is reinforced by the smell of melted cheddar and the crowded escalators to the different floors, where the masses float past old friends such Yves Klein or "Jack the Dripper" Pollock or *Unsupervised*, a huge digital sculpture by Turkish artist Refik Anadol whose concepts are interesting, although I can't help feeling reminded of an aquarium at *Changi Airport* in Singapore.

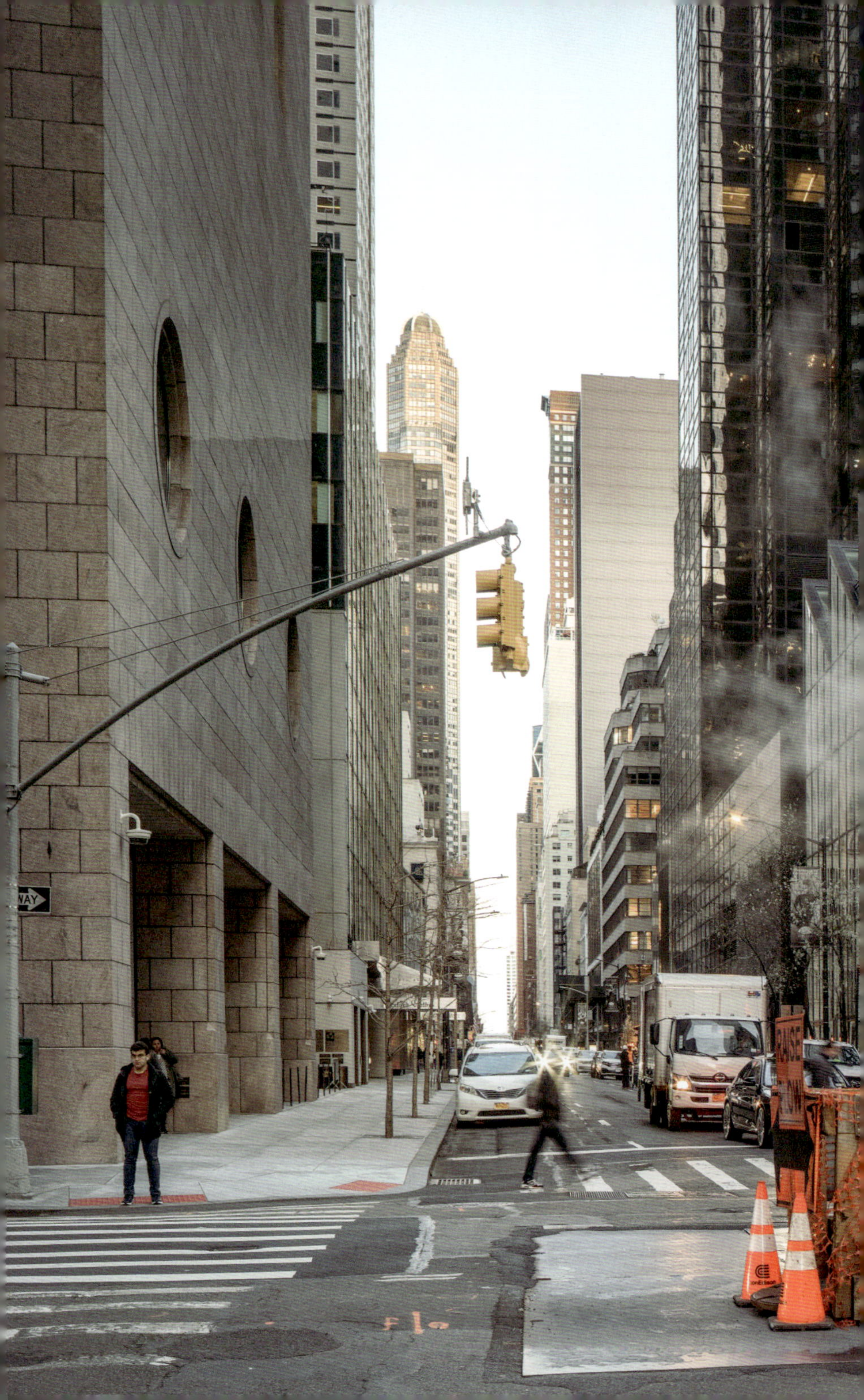
WAY
RAISE

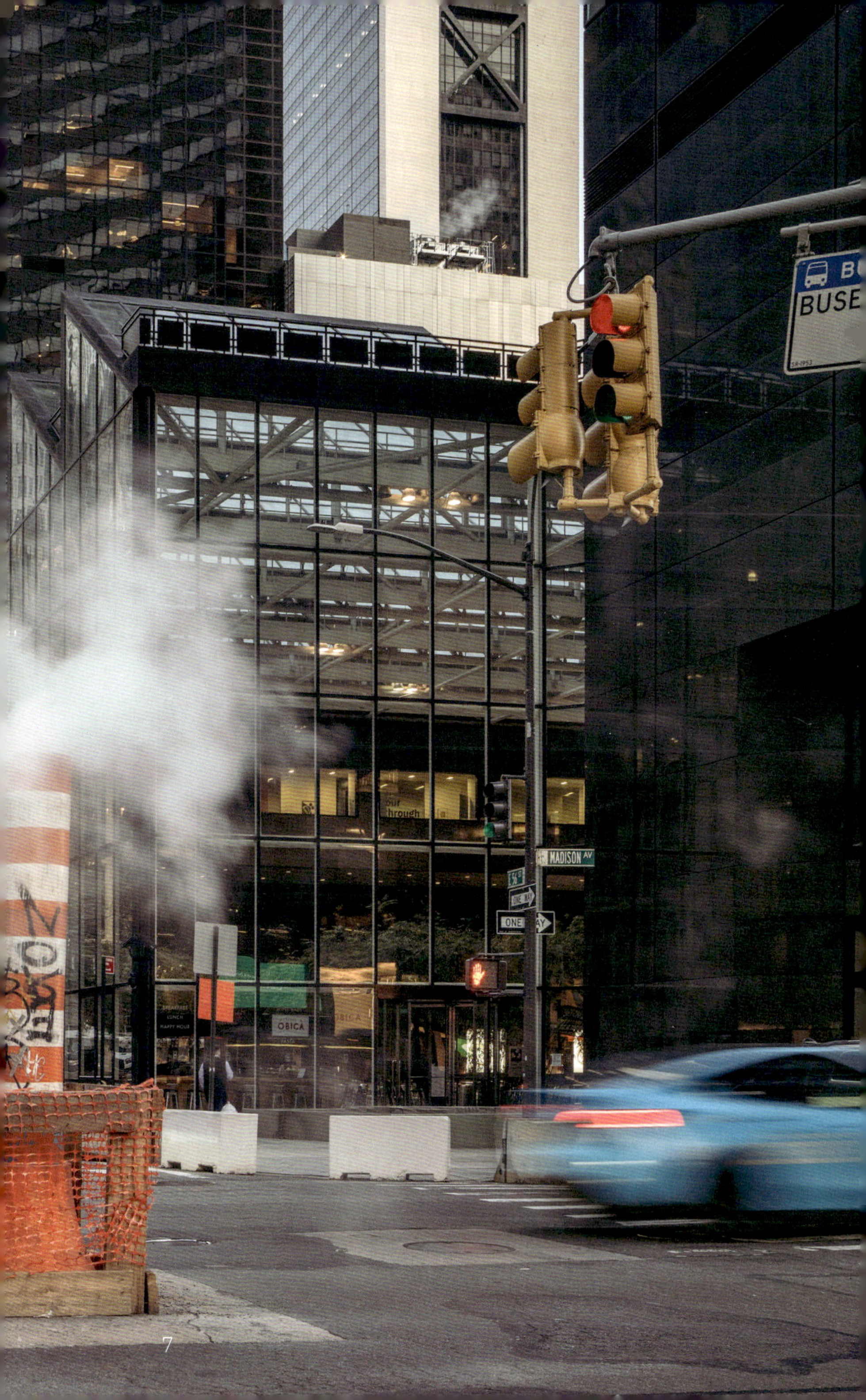
BUSE
MADISON AV
ONE WAY
OBICA

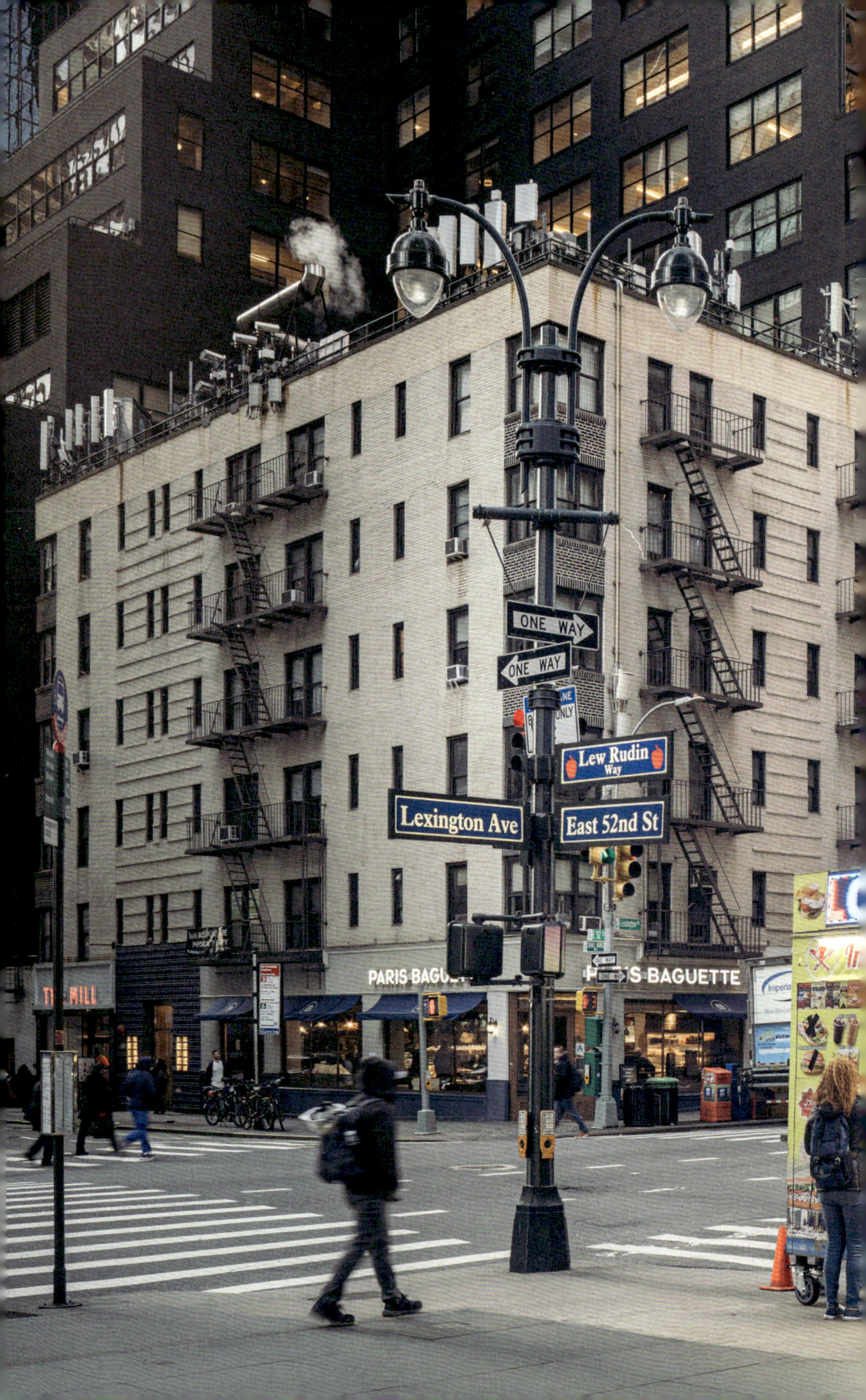
ONE WAY
ONE WAY
Lew Rudin
Way
Lexington Ave
East 52nd St
PARIS BAGUETTE
THE MILL

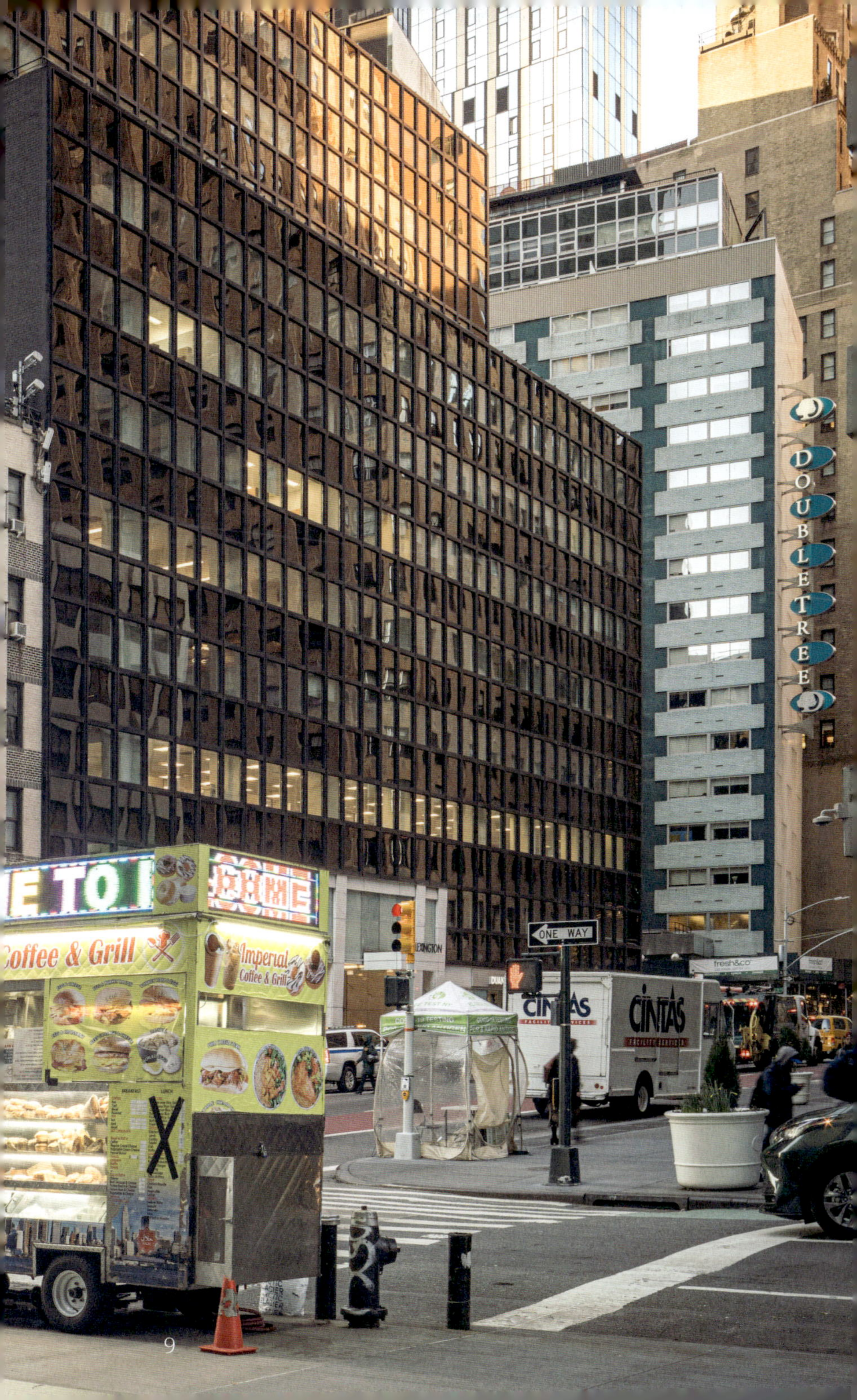
DOUBLETREE
ONE WAY
Coffee & Grill
Imperial
Coffee & Grill
CINTAS
CINTAS

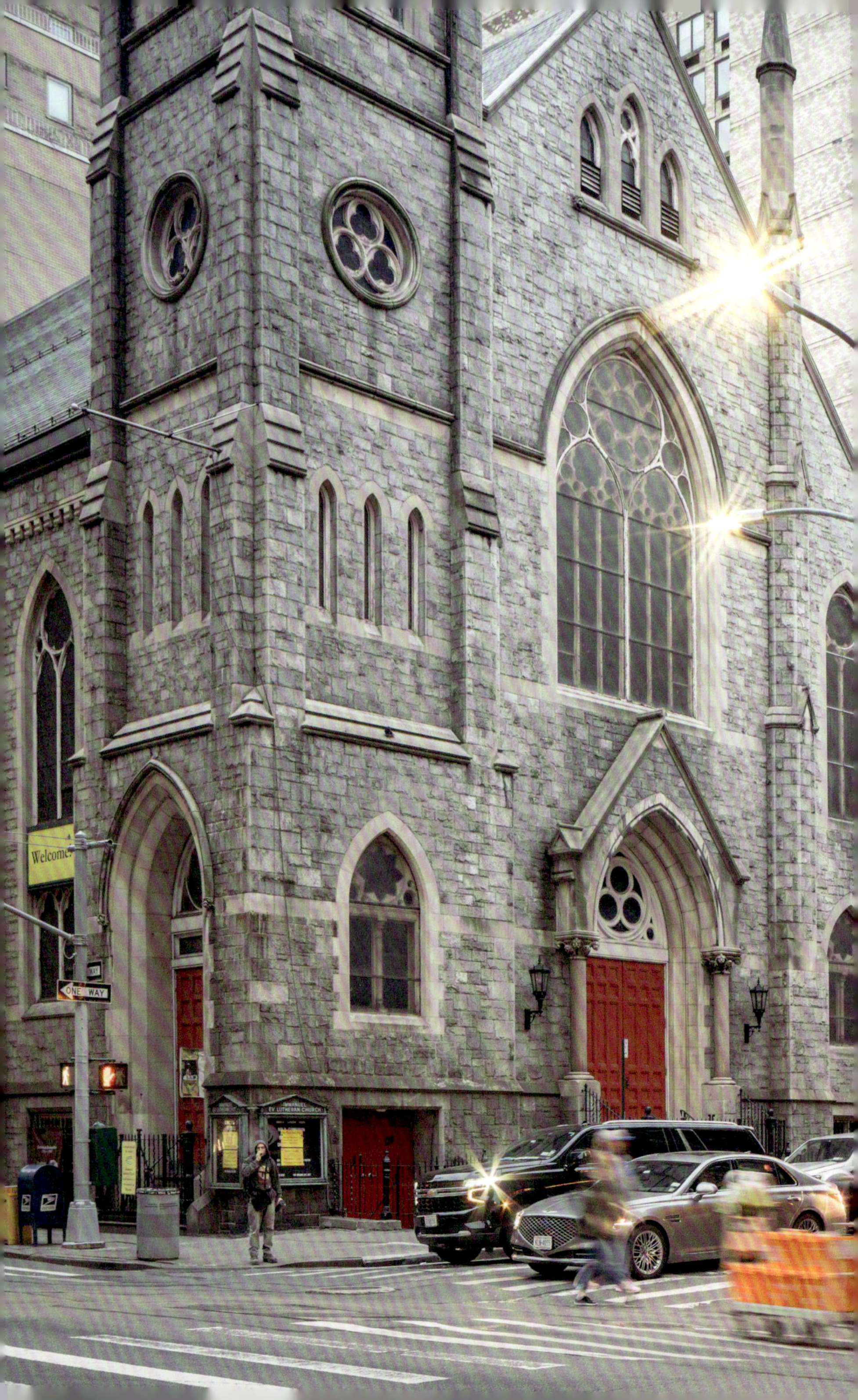
Welcome
ONE WAY

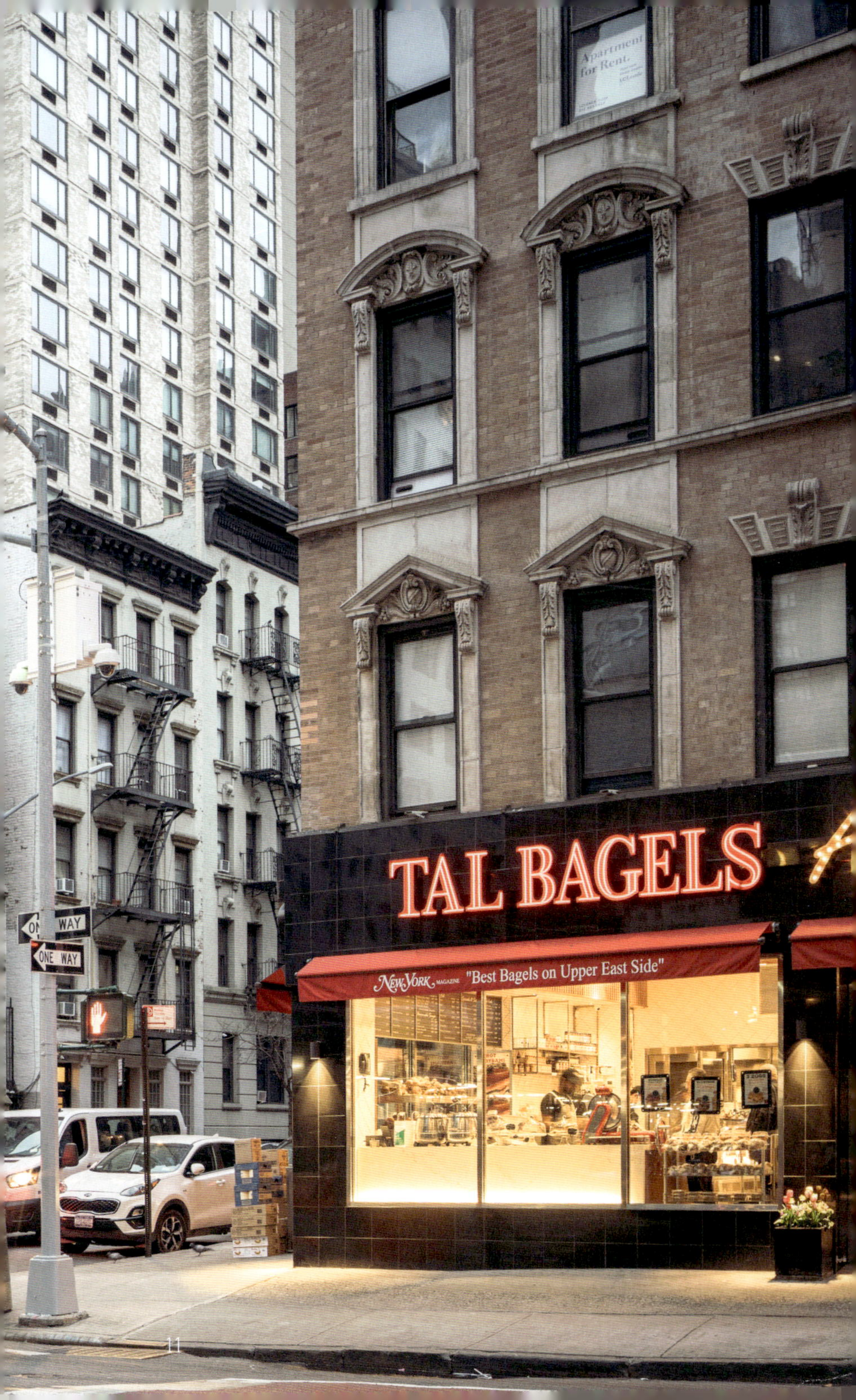
Apartment for Rent.
TAL BAGELS
New York MAGAZINE "Best Bagels on Upper East Side"
ONE WAY

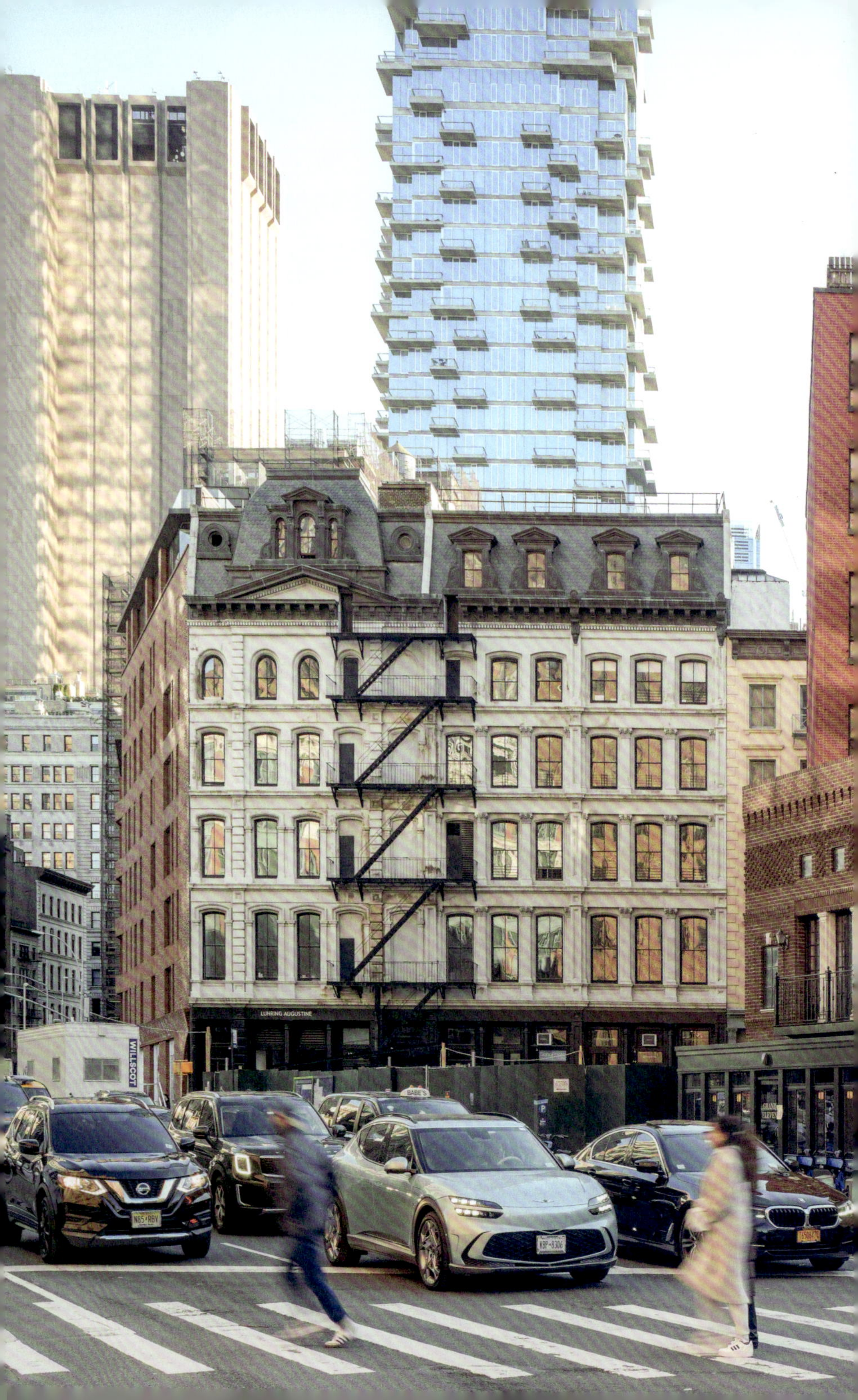
LUHRING AUGUSTINE
WILLSCOT

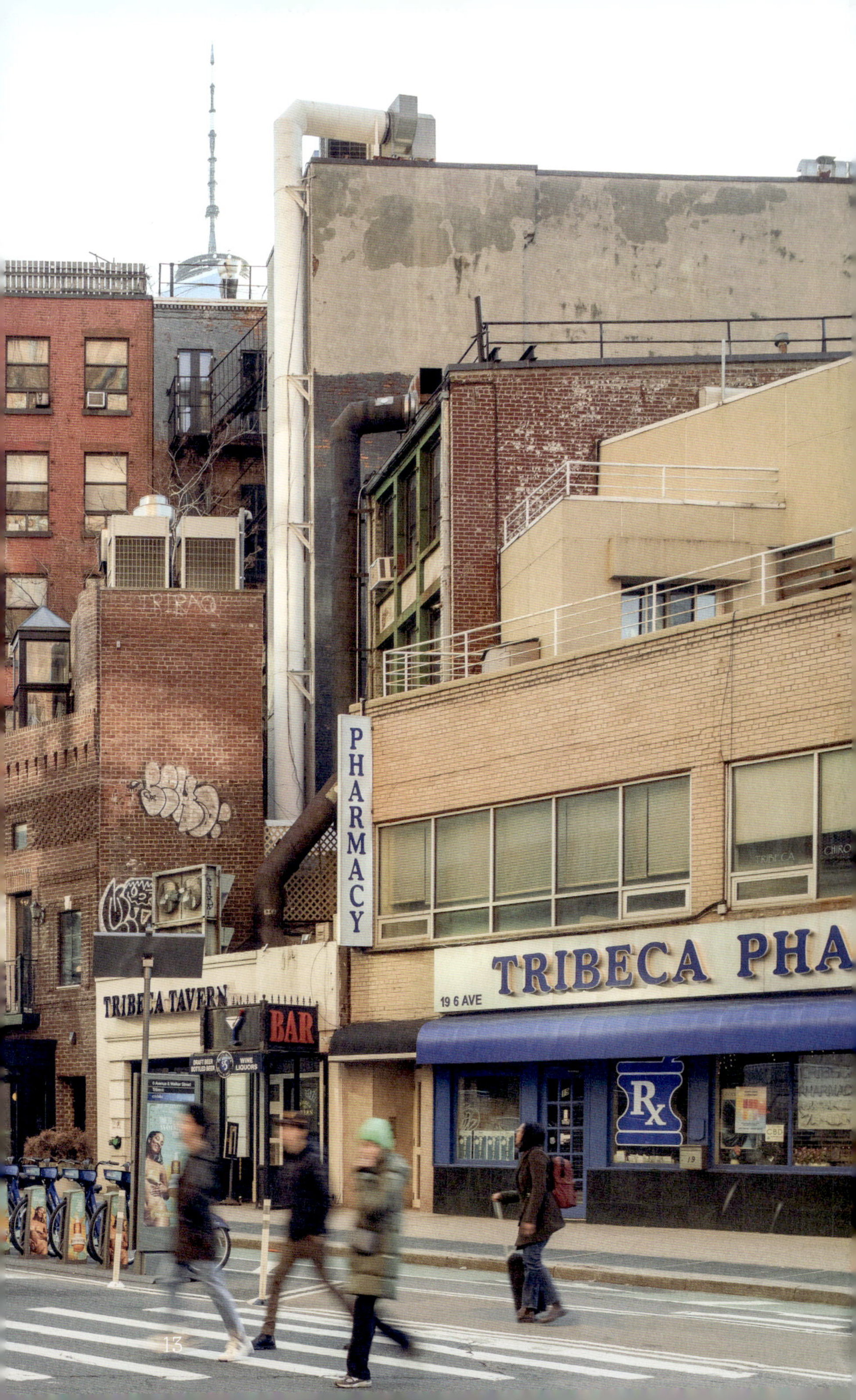
PHARMACY
TRIBECA PHA
19 6 AVE
TRIBECA TAVERN
BAR
Rx

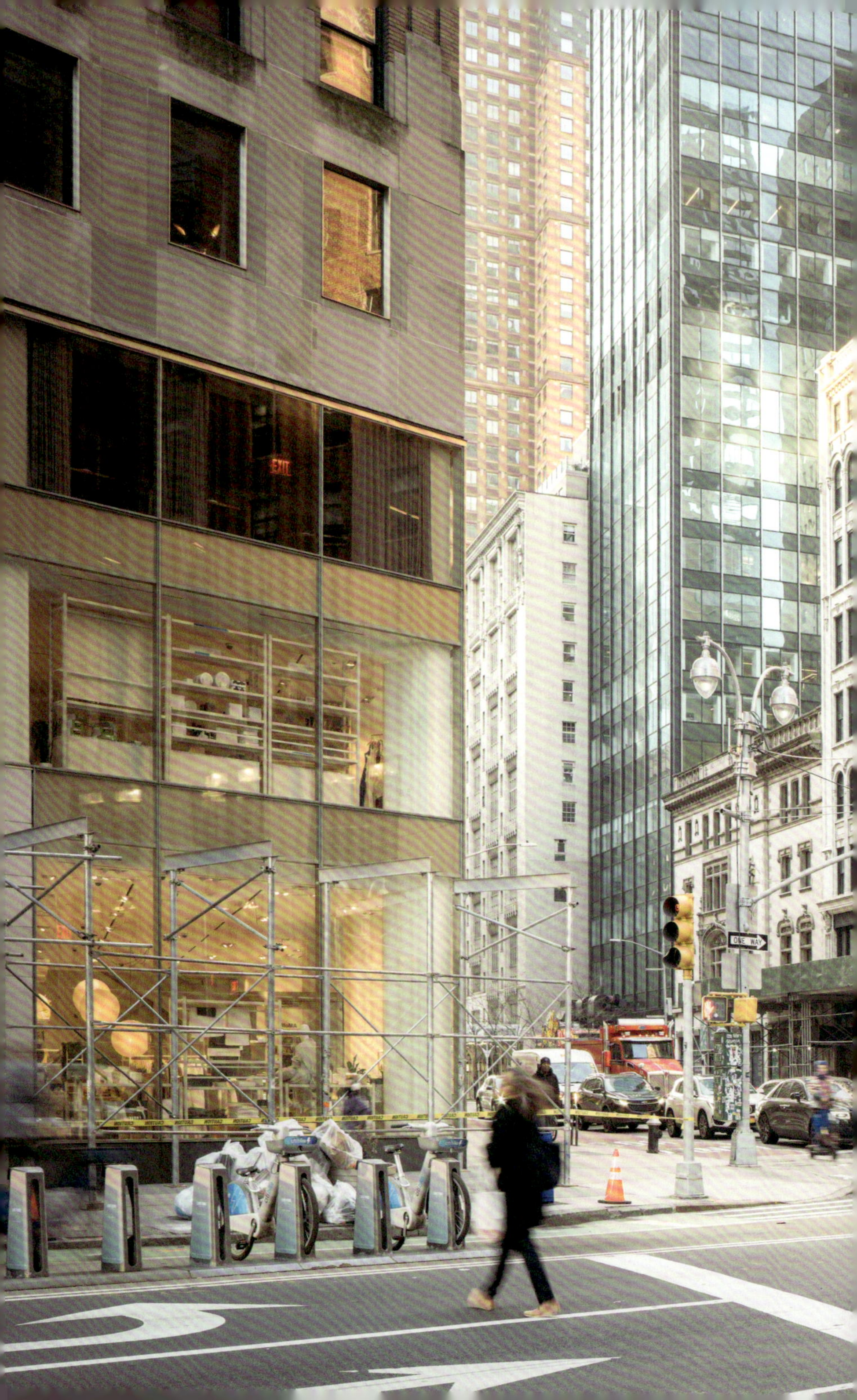
EXIT
ONE WAY

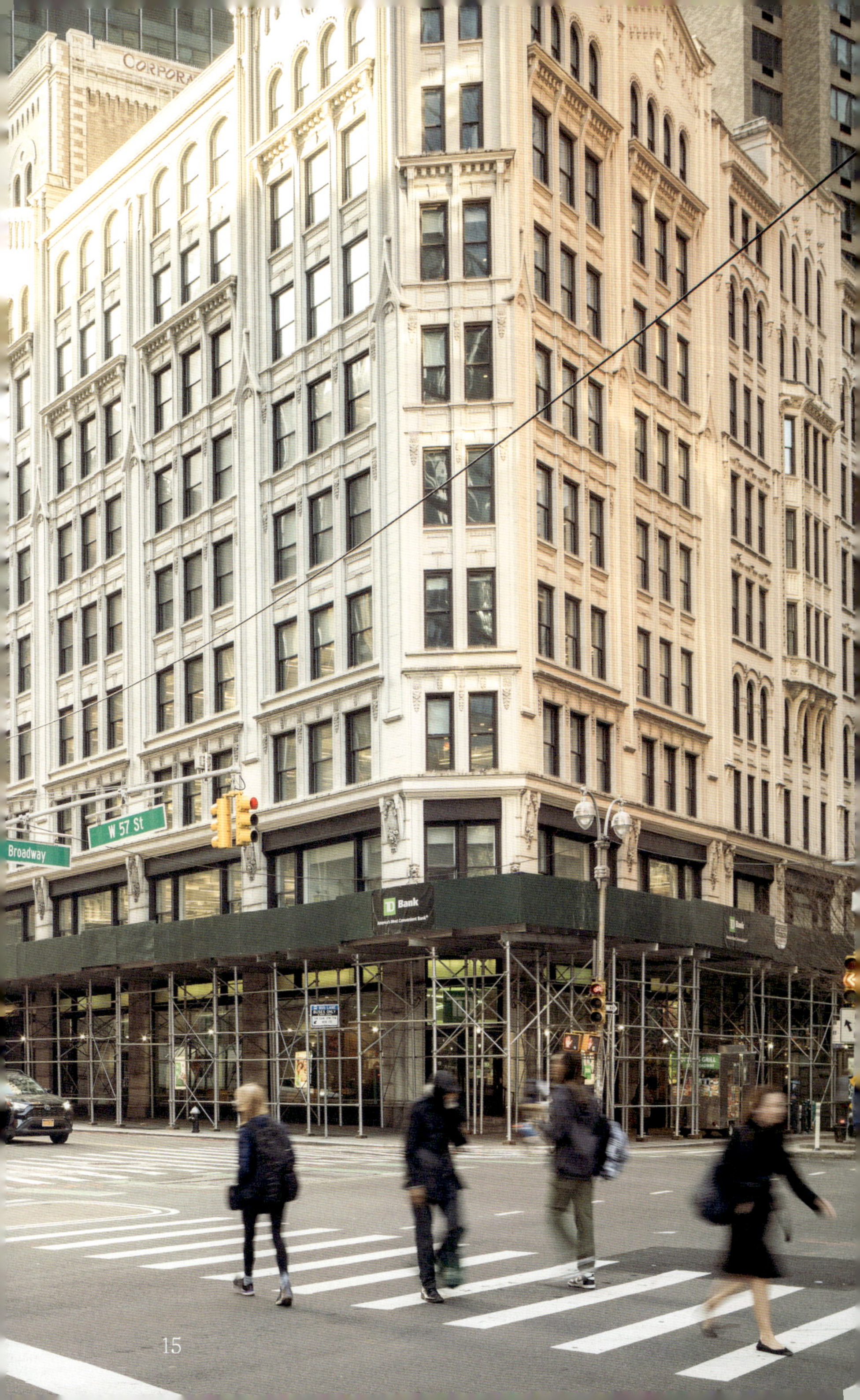
W 57 St
Broadway
TD Bank

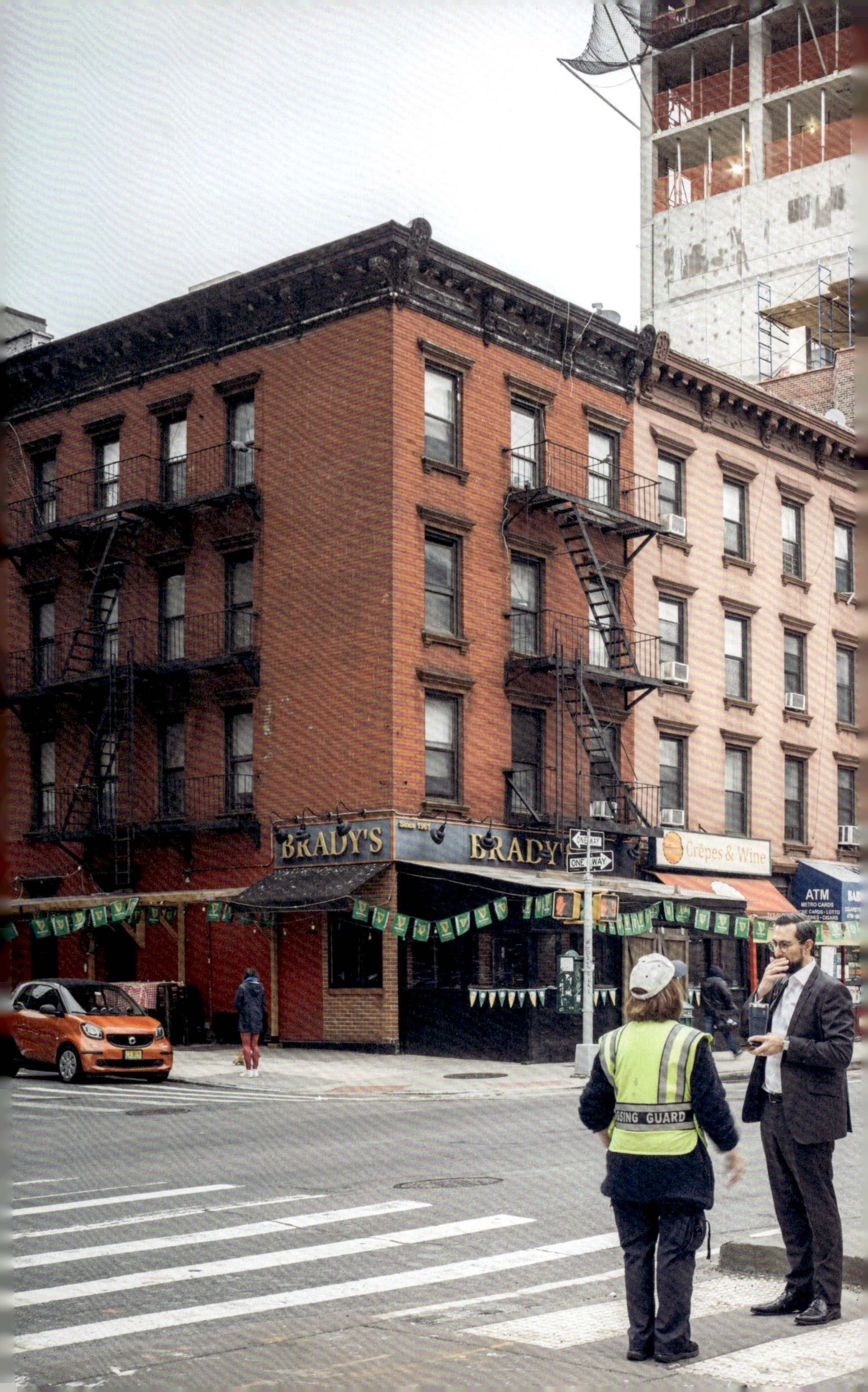
BRADY'S
Since 1961
ONE WAY
ONE WAY
Crêpes & Wine
ATM
METRO CARDS

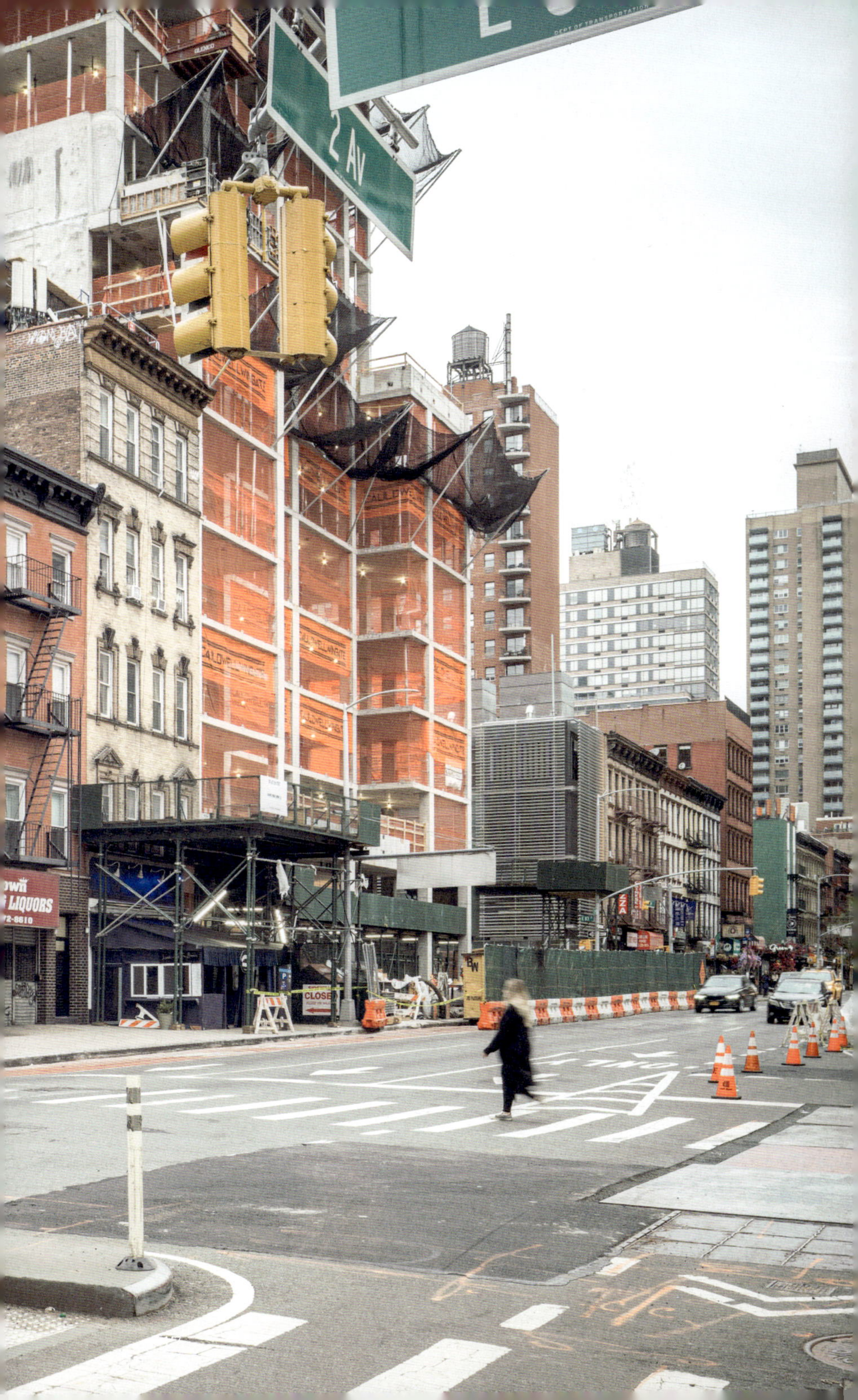
2 Av
LIQUORS
CLOSE

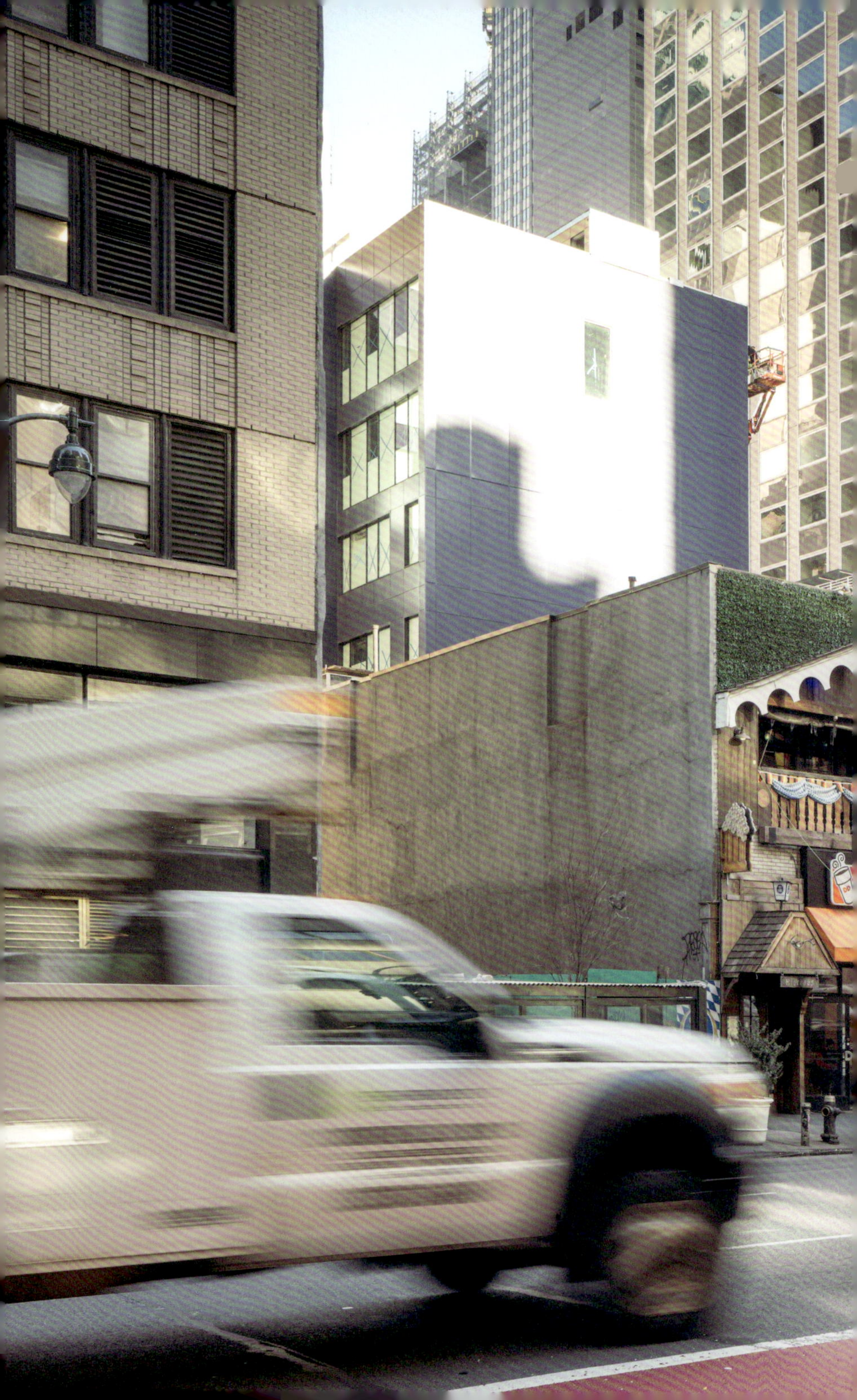

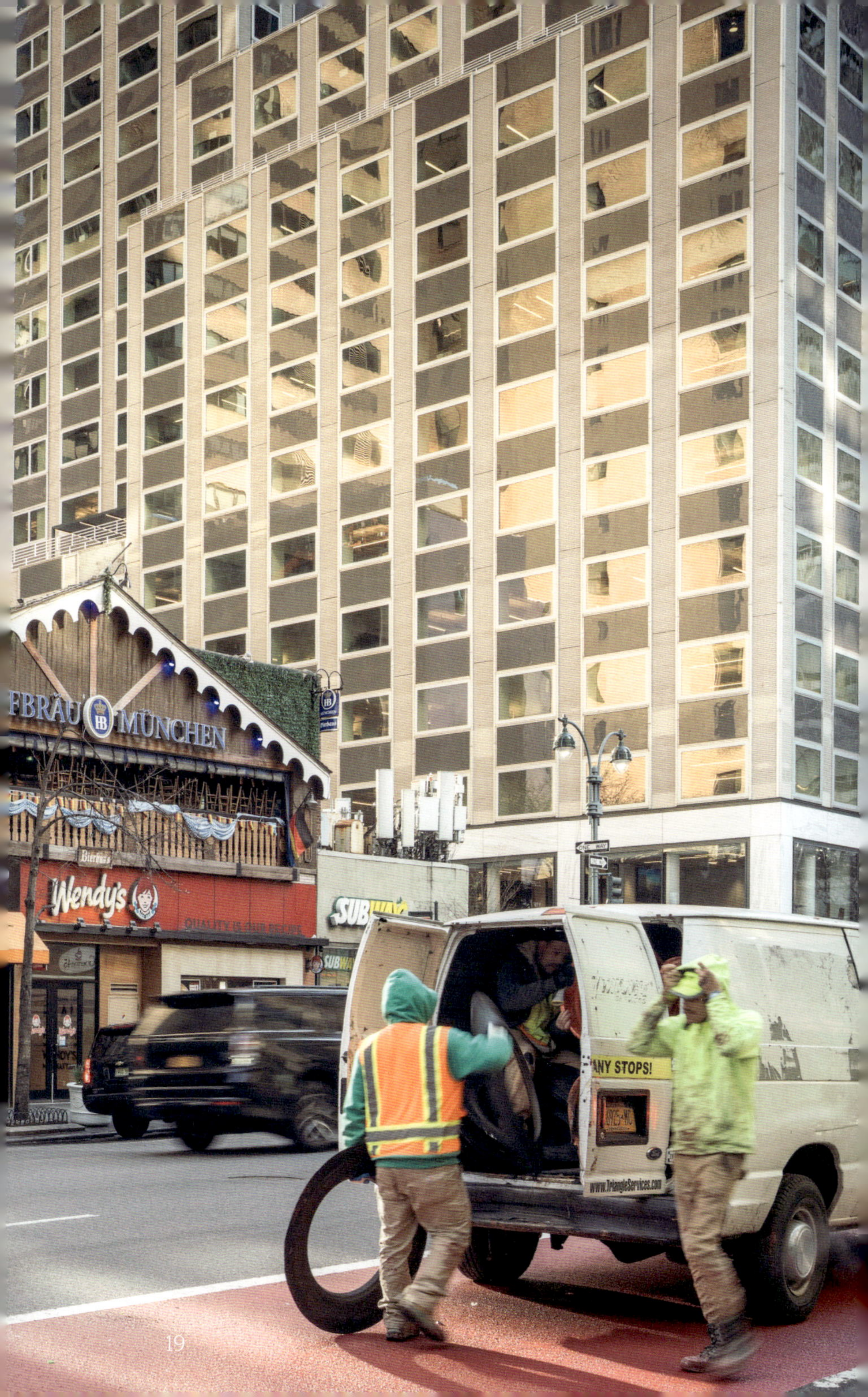
FBRÄU
MÜNCHEN
Wendy's
ANY STOPS!
www.TriangleServices.com

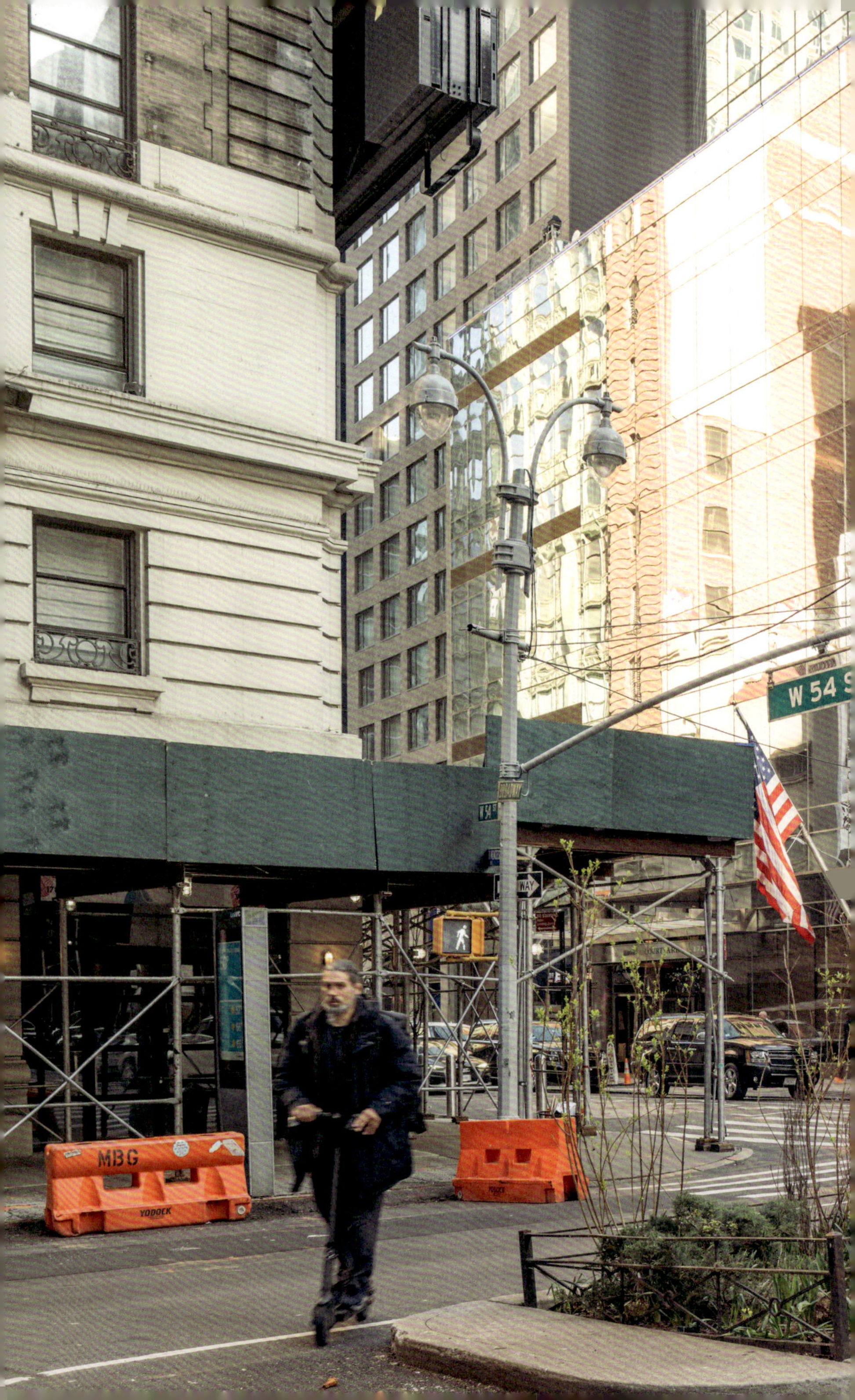
W 54 S
MBG
YODOCK

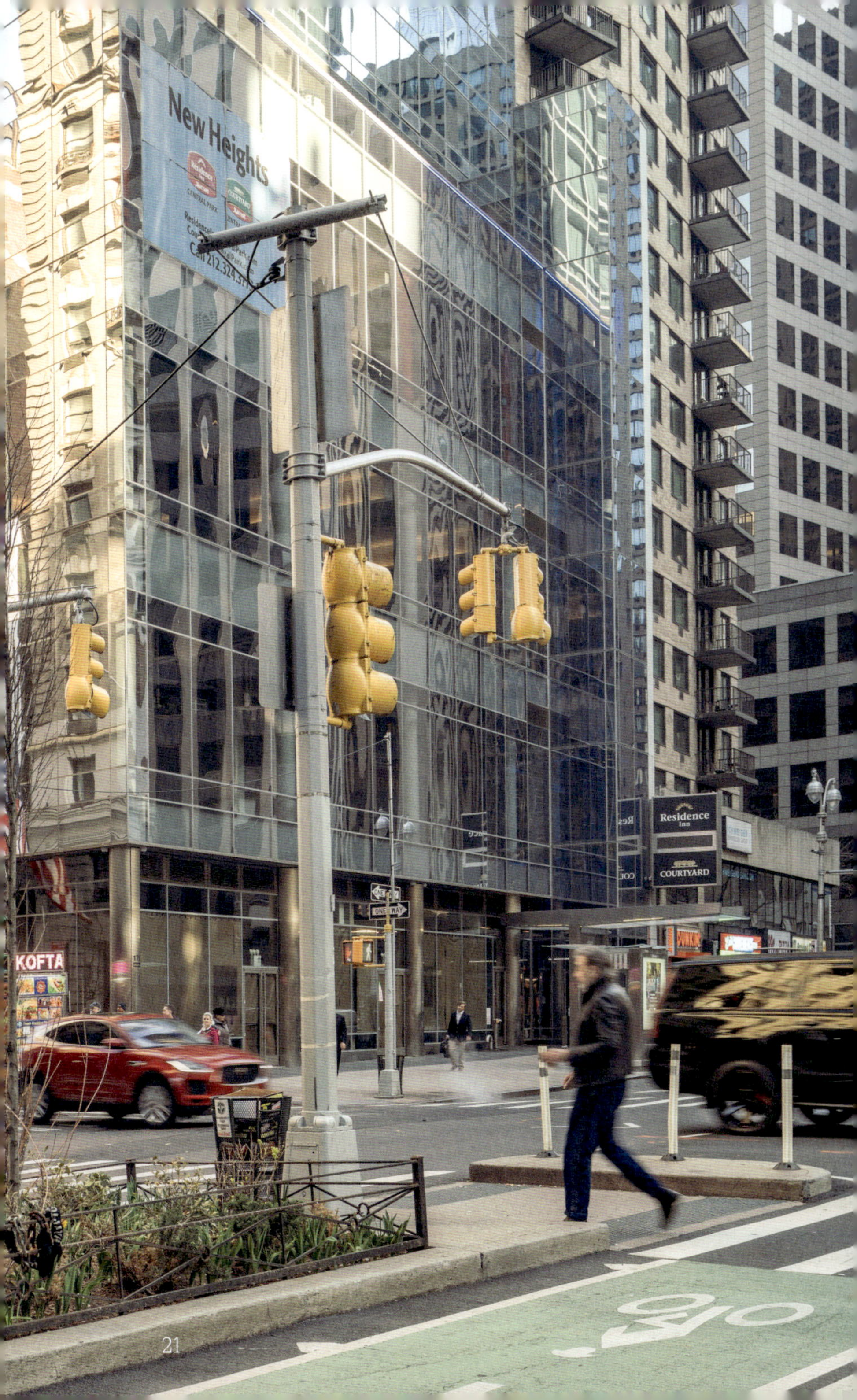
New Heights
Residence Inn
COURTYARD
KOFTA
ONE WAY

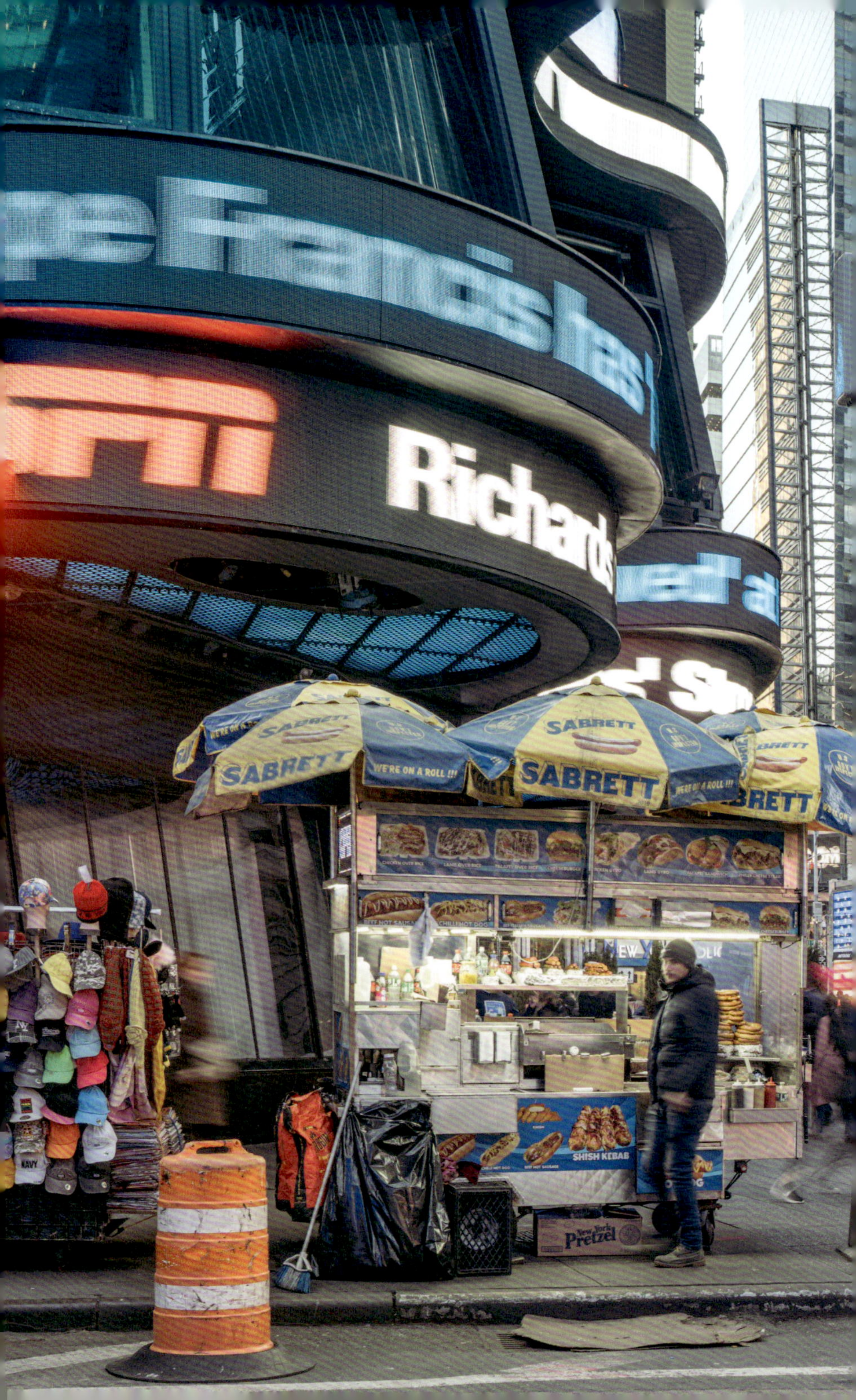
Richards
SABRETT
WE'RE ON A ROLL !!!
SABRETT
SHISH KEBAB
New York Pretzel

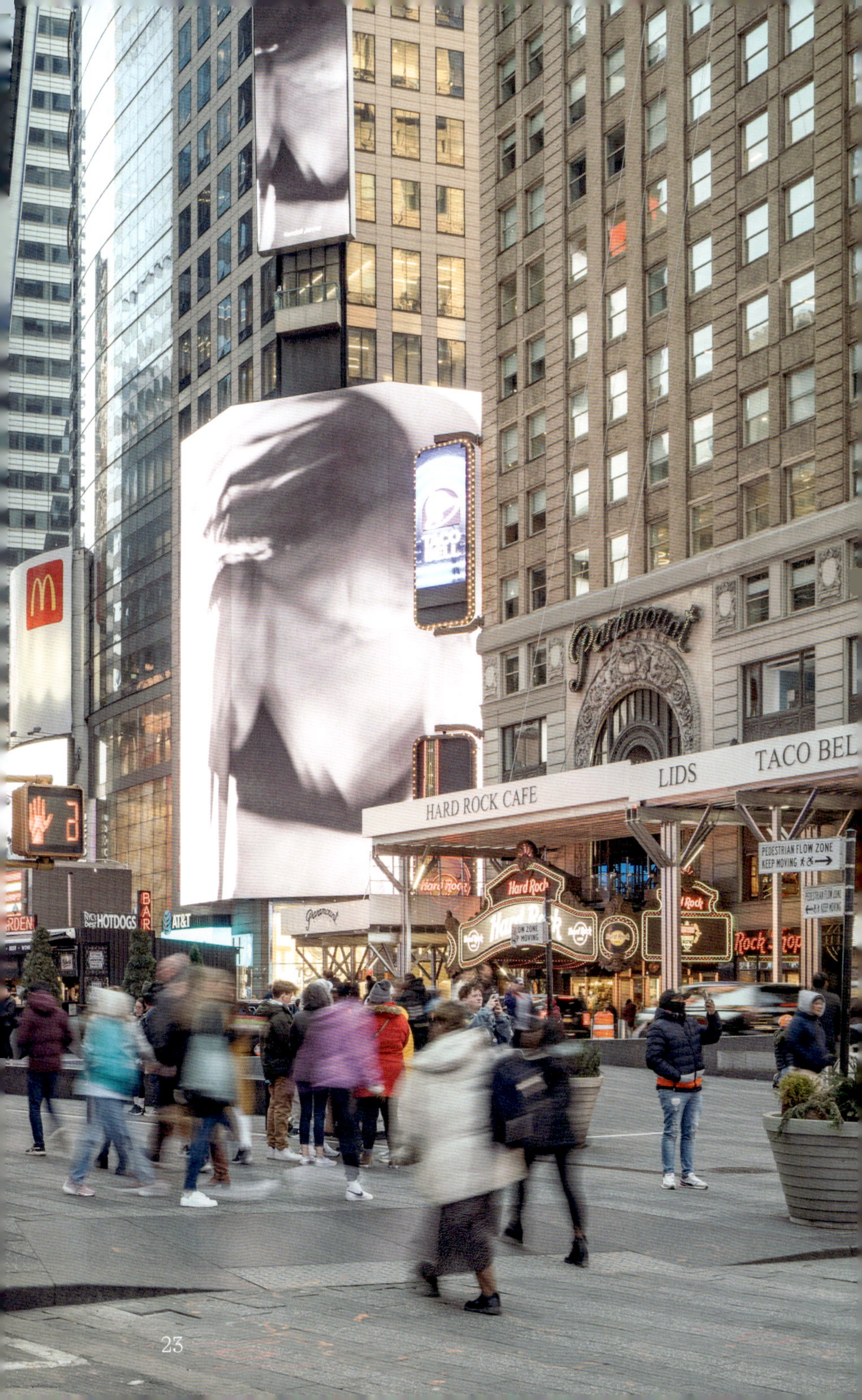
Paramount
TACO BELL
HARD ROCK CAFE
LIDS
TACO BEL
PEDESTRIAN FLOW ZONE
KEEP MOVING
Hard Rock
HOTDOGS
BAR
AT&T

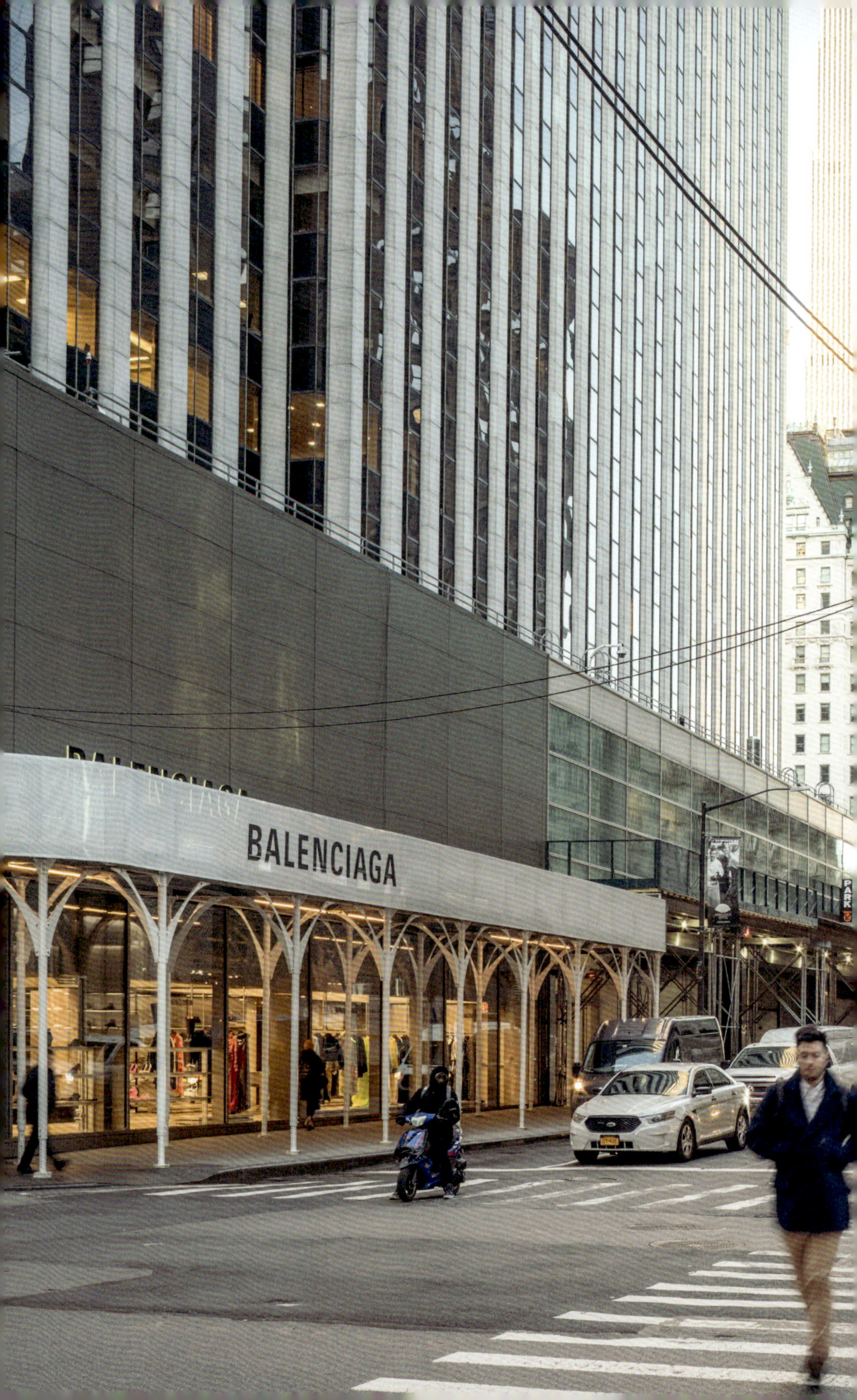
BALENCIAGA

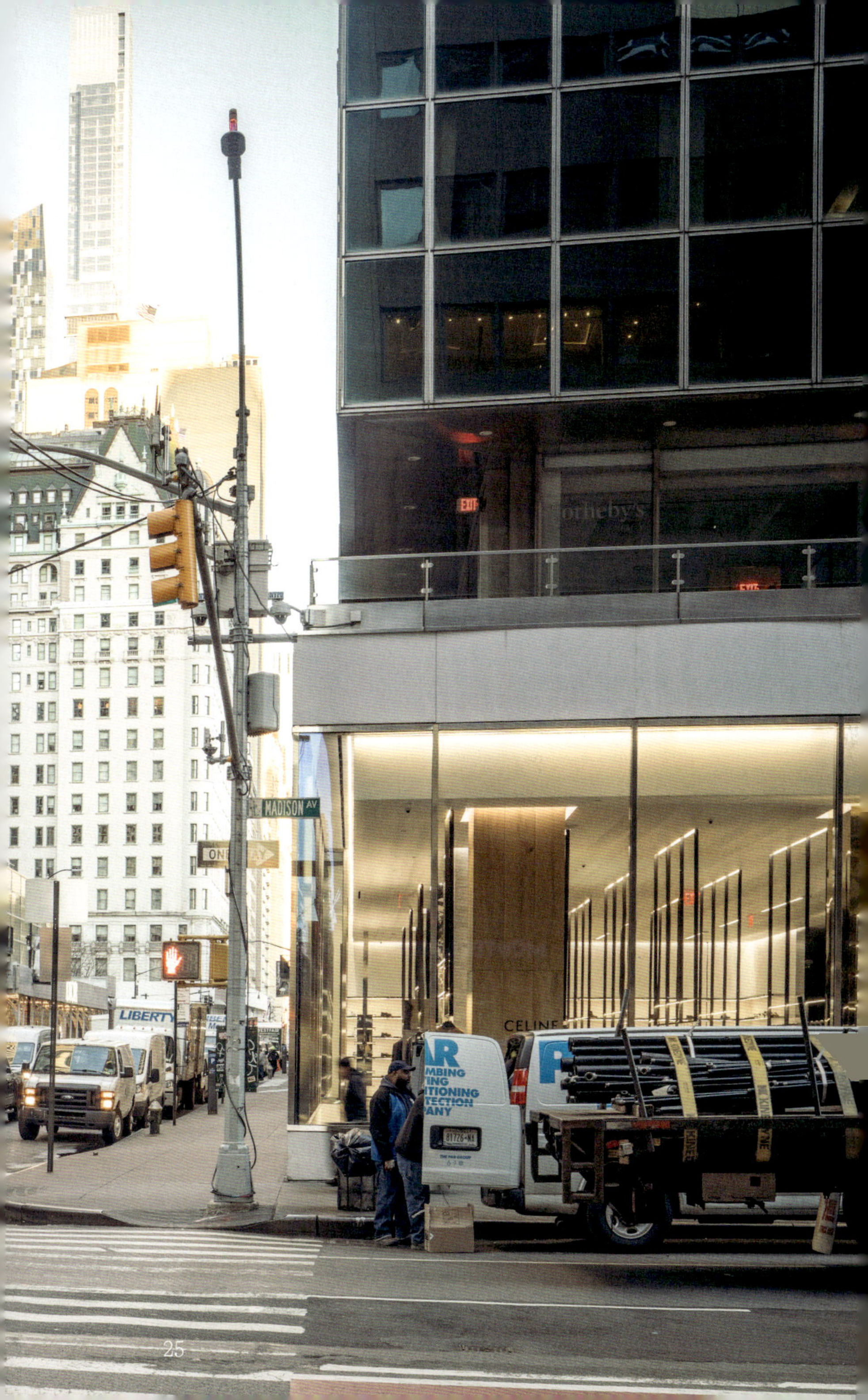
MADISON AV
EXIT
CELINE
LIBERTY

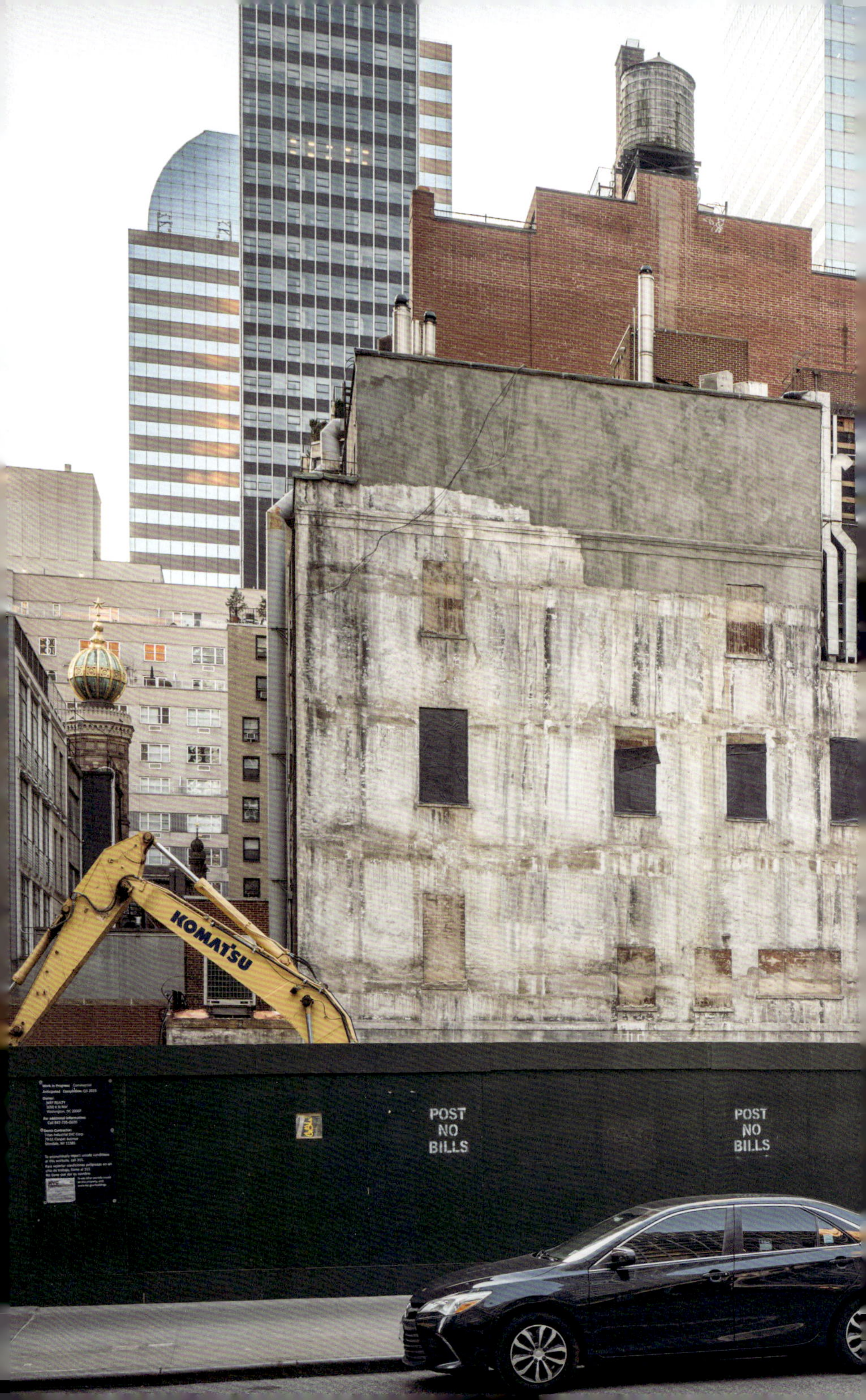
KOMATSU
POST
NO
BILLS
POST
NO
BILLS

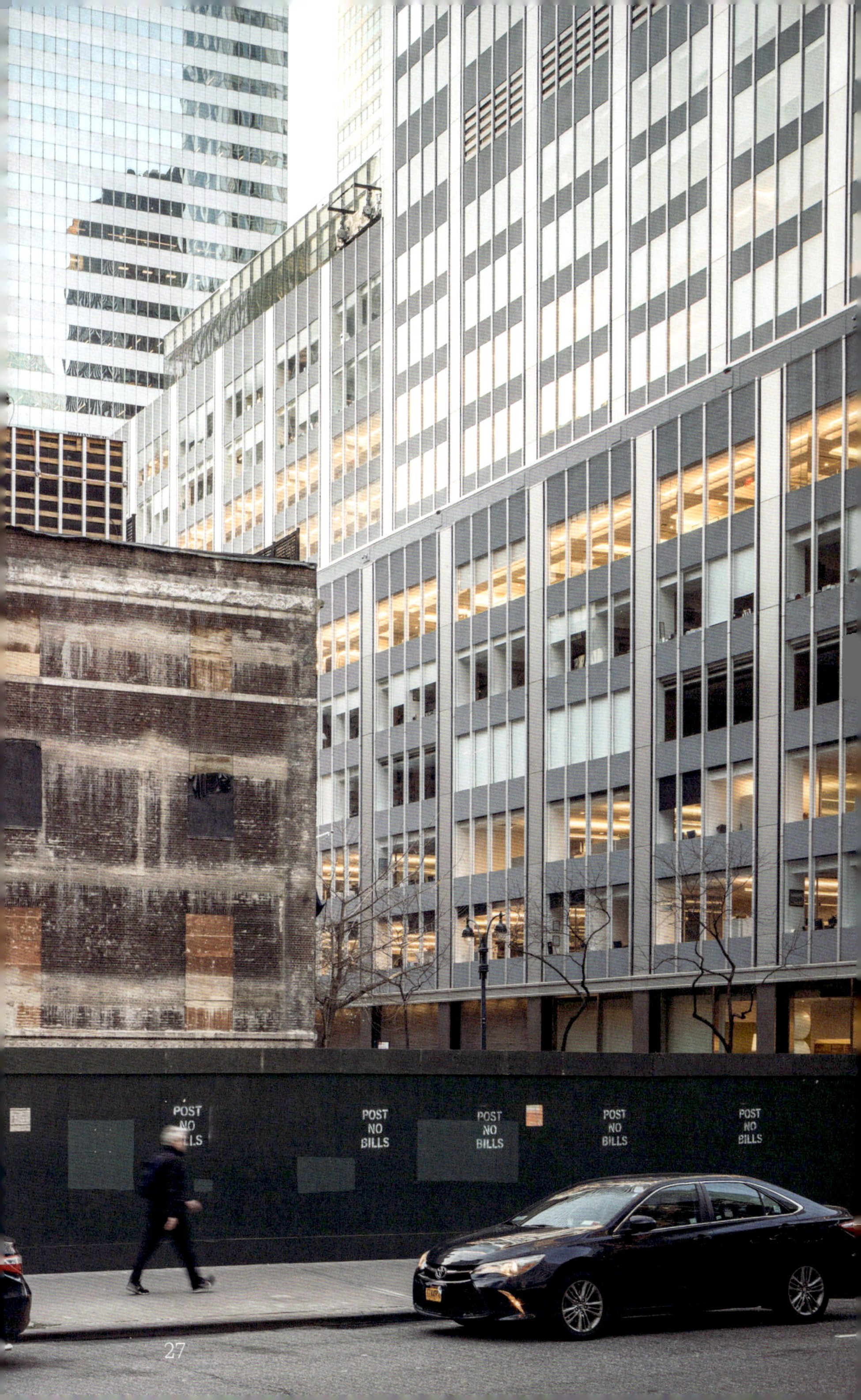
POST
NO
BILLS
POST
NO
BILLS
POST
NO
BILLS
POST
NO
BILLS

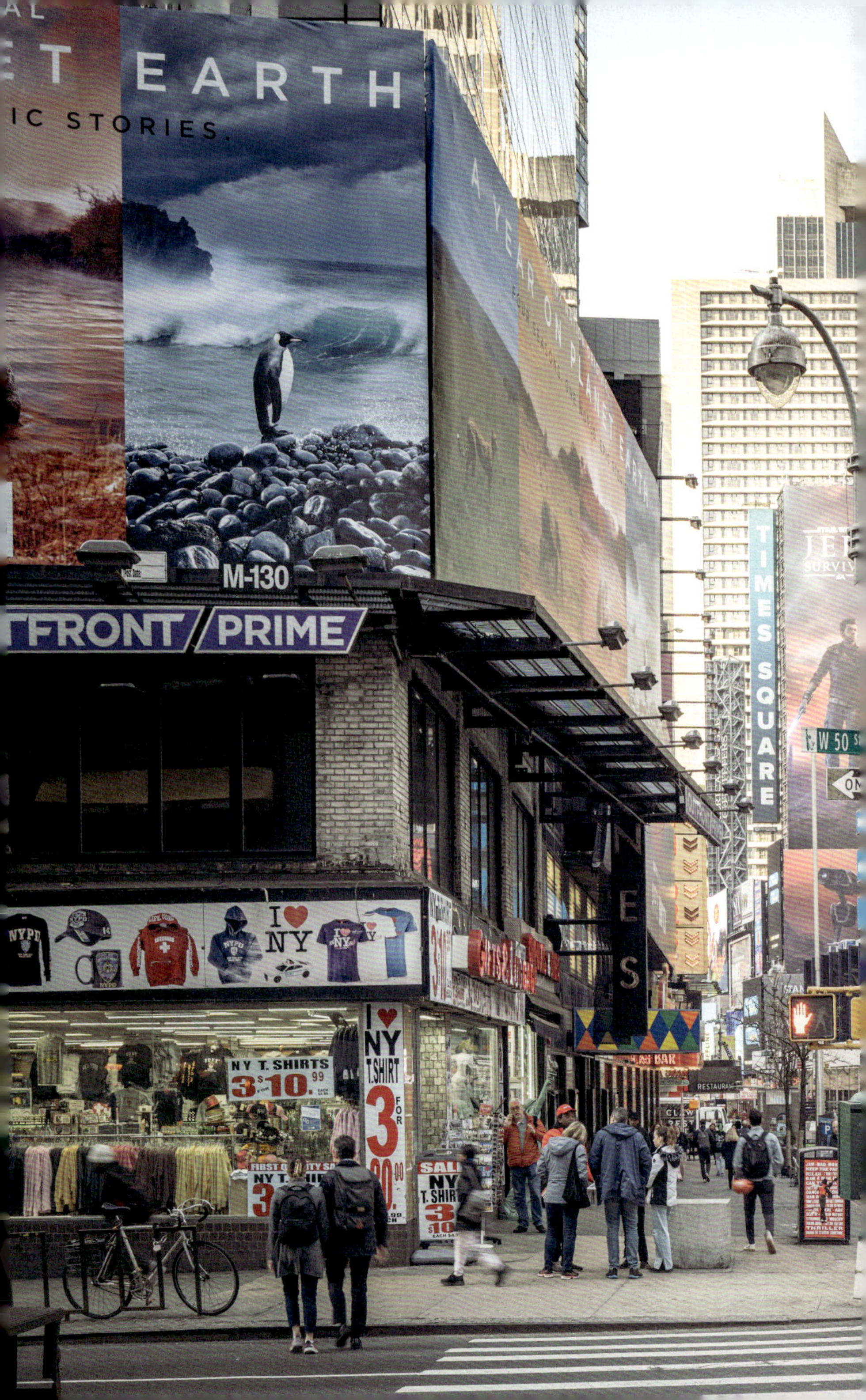
EARTH
IC STORIES.
A YEAR ON PLANET EARTH
M-130
FRONT
PRIME
TIMES SQUARE
I ♥ NY
NYPD
N Y T. SHIRTS
3 FOR $10.99
I ♥ NY T.SHIRT 3 FOR
RESTAURANT

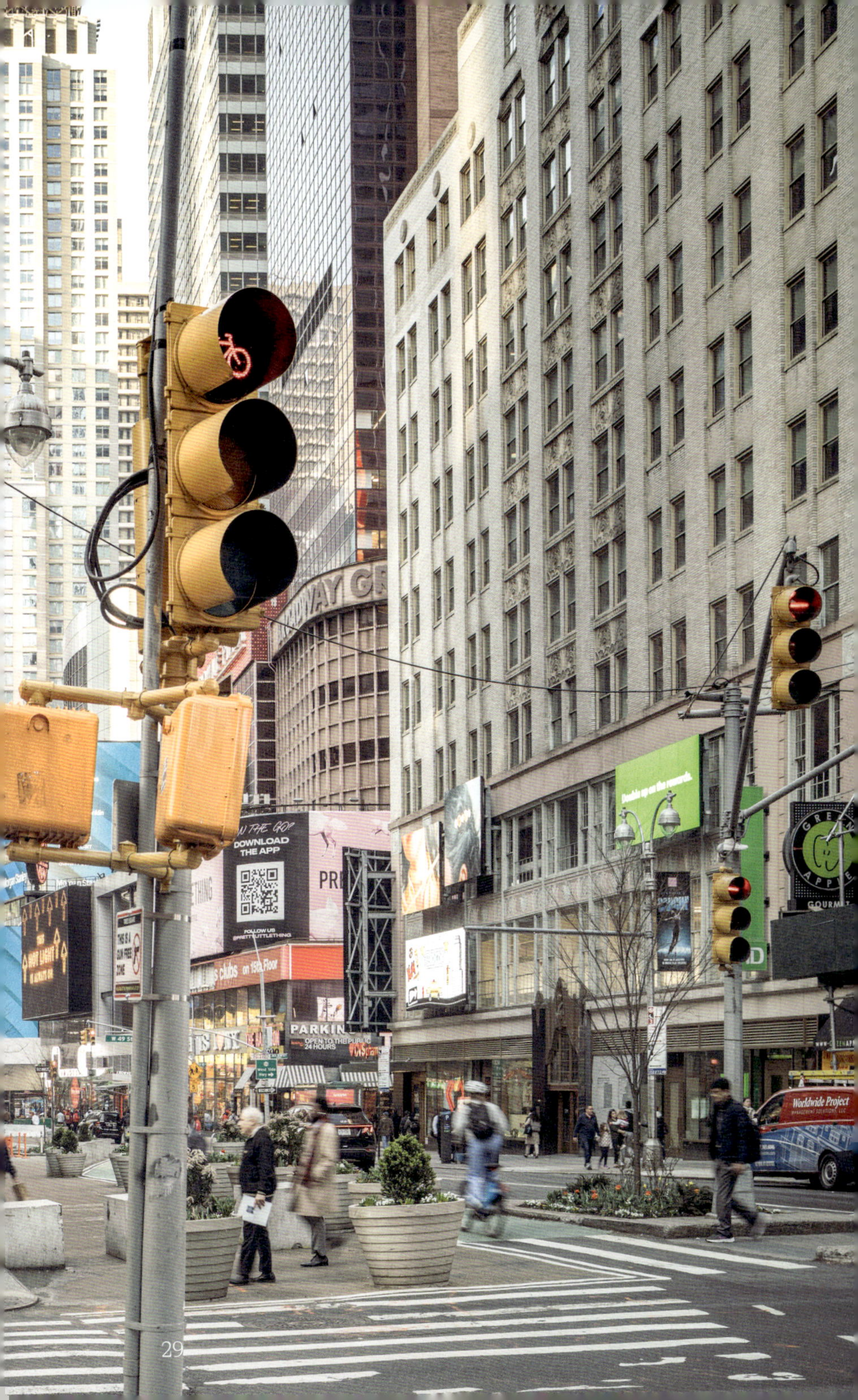
DOWNLOAD THE APP
OPEN TO THE PUBLIC 24 HOURS
Worldwide Project

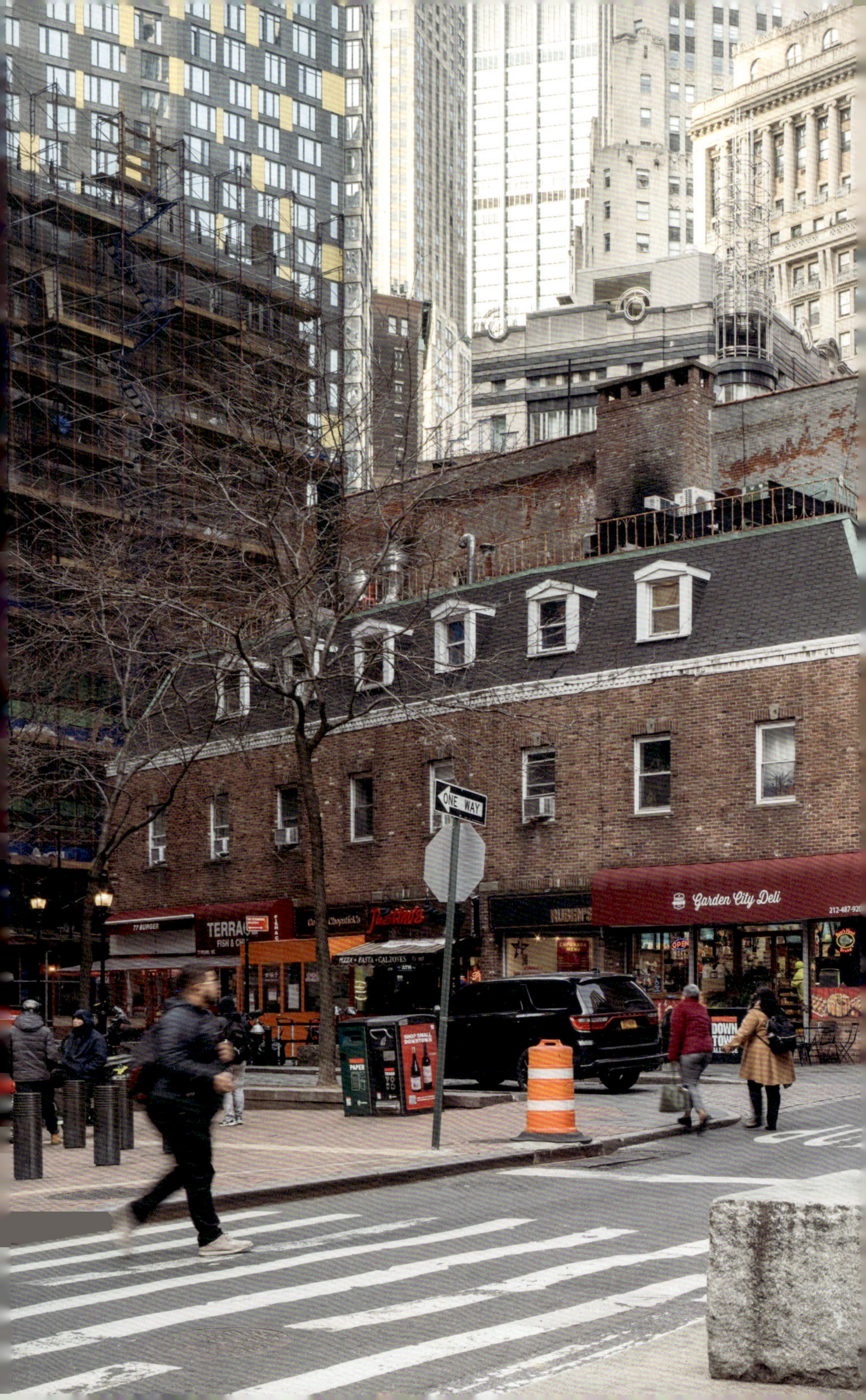
ONE WAY
Garden City Deli
77 BURGER

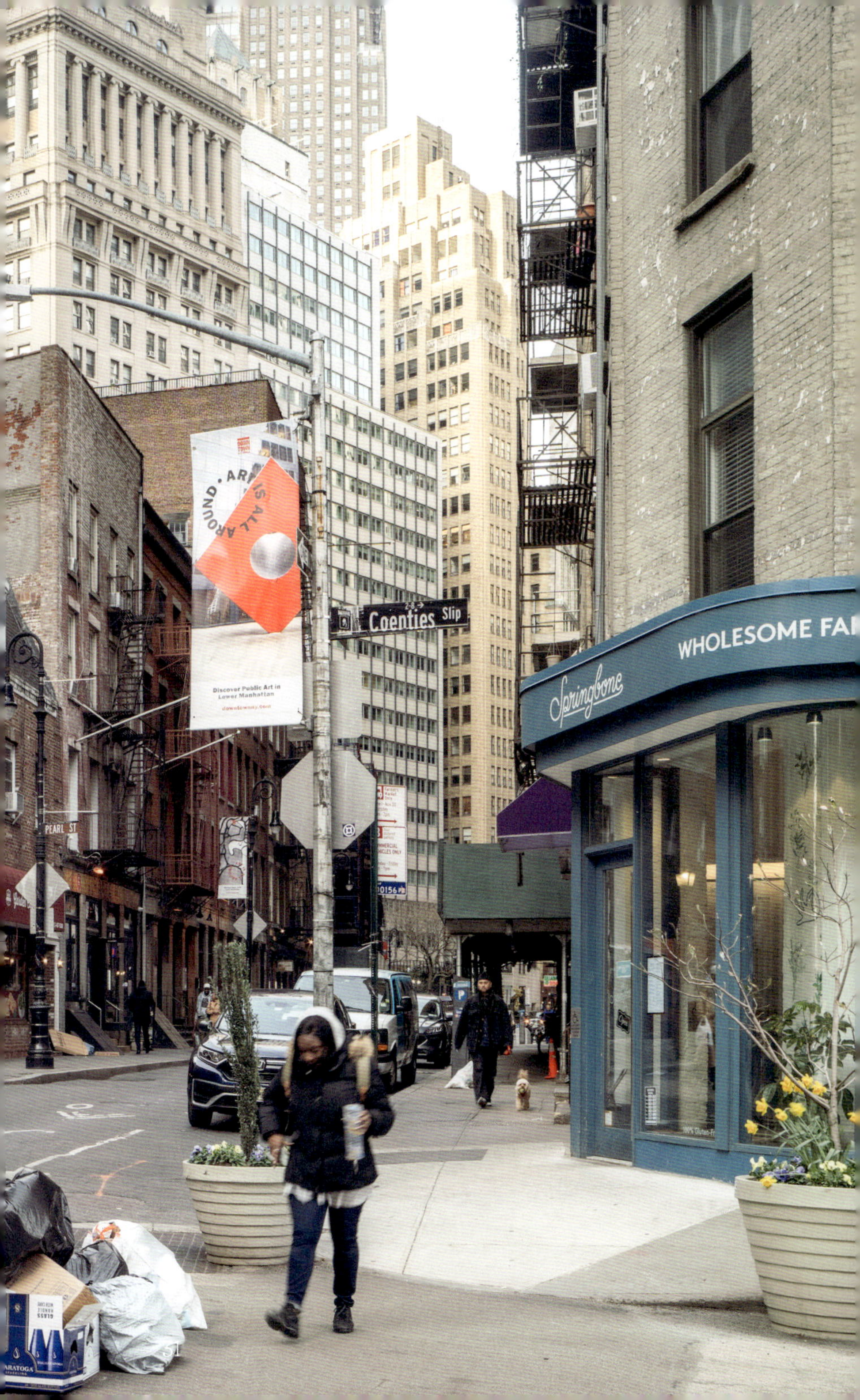

Coenties Slip
WHOLESOME FA
Springbone
PEARL ST
Discover Public Art in Lower Manhattan

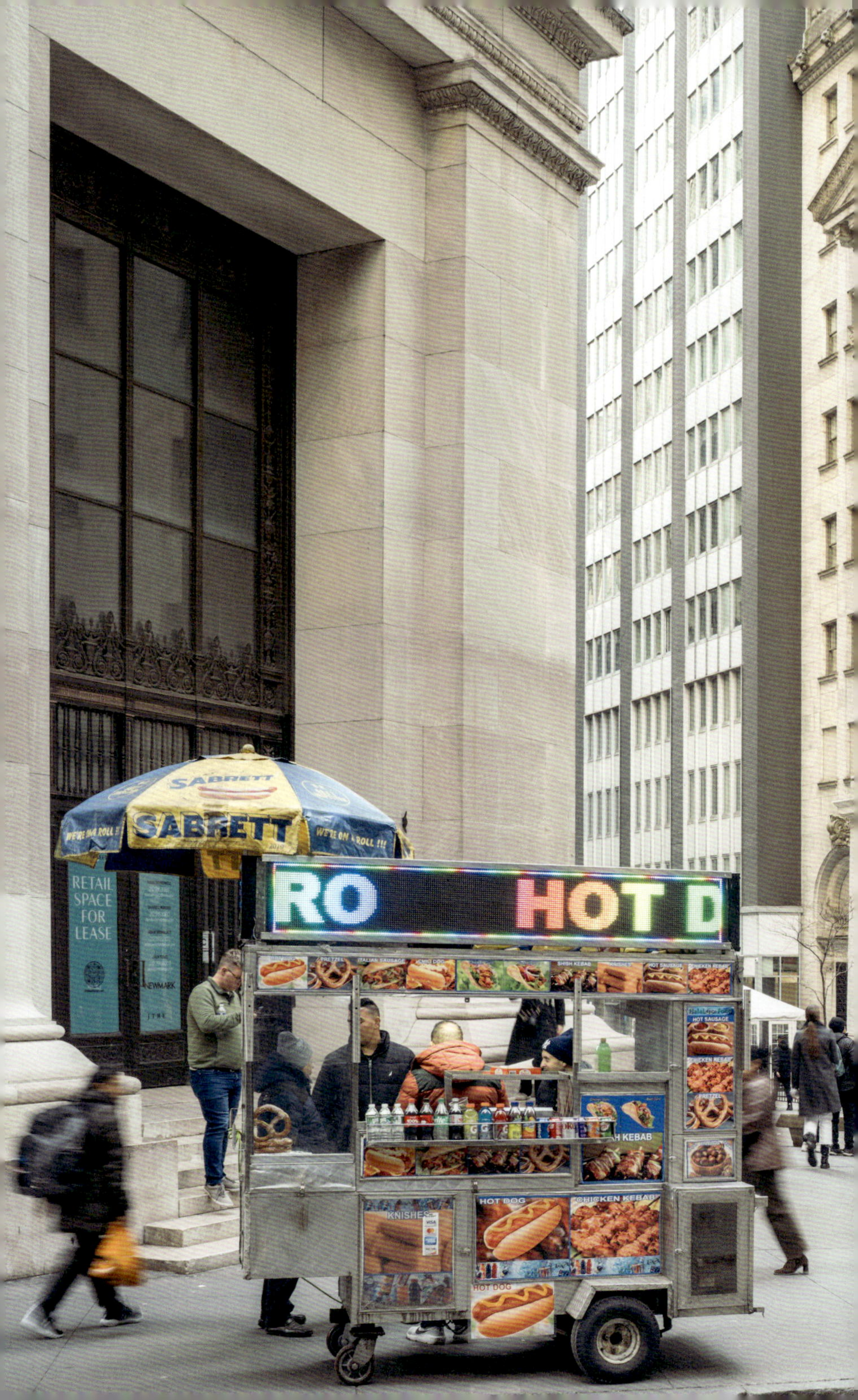
SABRETT
WE'RE ON A ROLL !!!
RETAIL SPACE FOR LEASE
NEWMARK
RO HOT D
HOT SAUSAGE
PRETZEL
H KEBAB
HOT DOG
CHICKEN KEBAB
KNISHES
HOT DOG

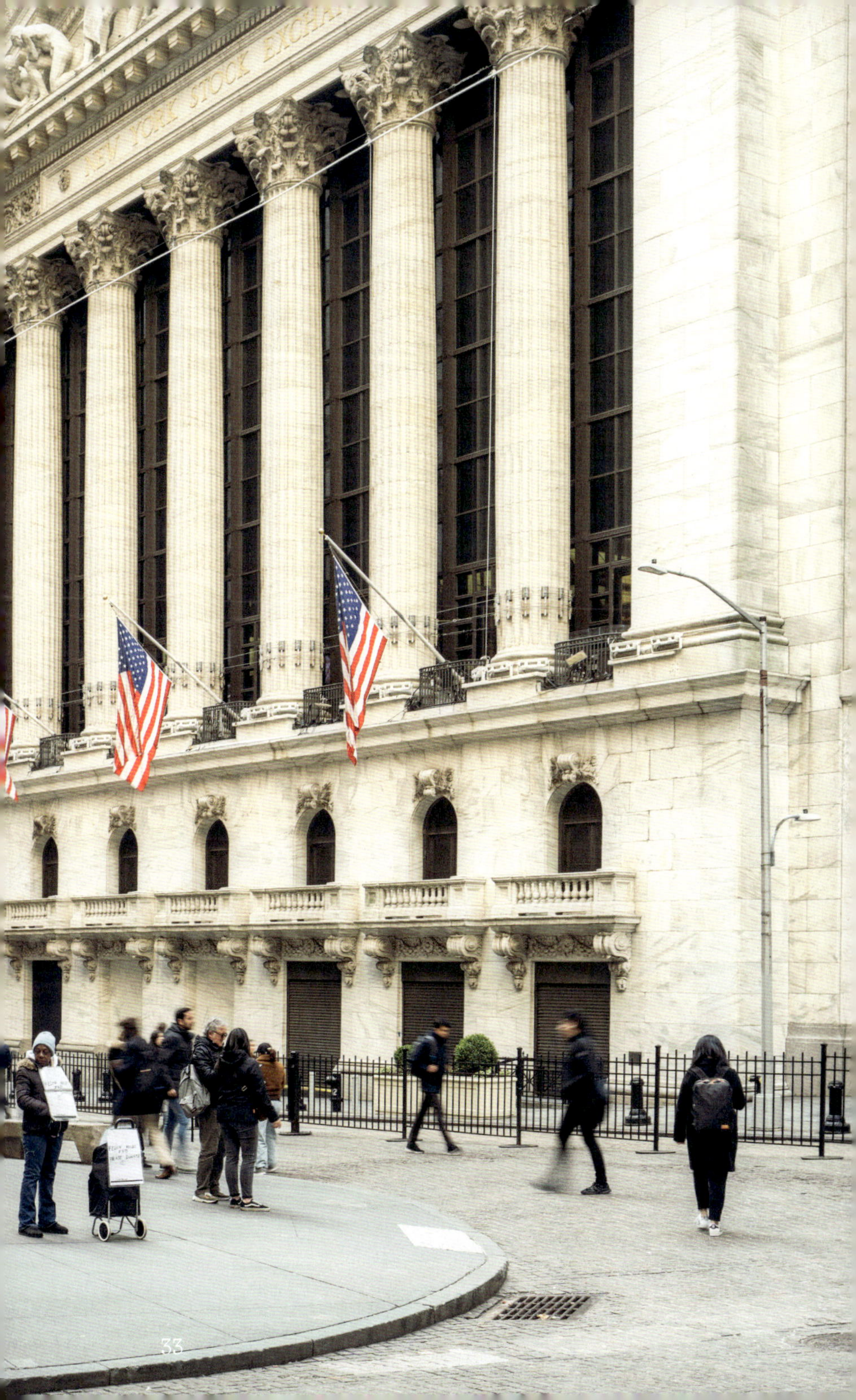

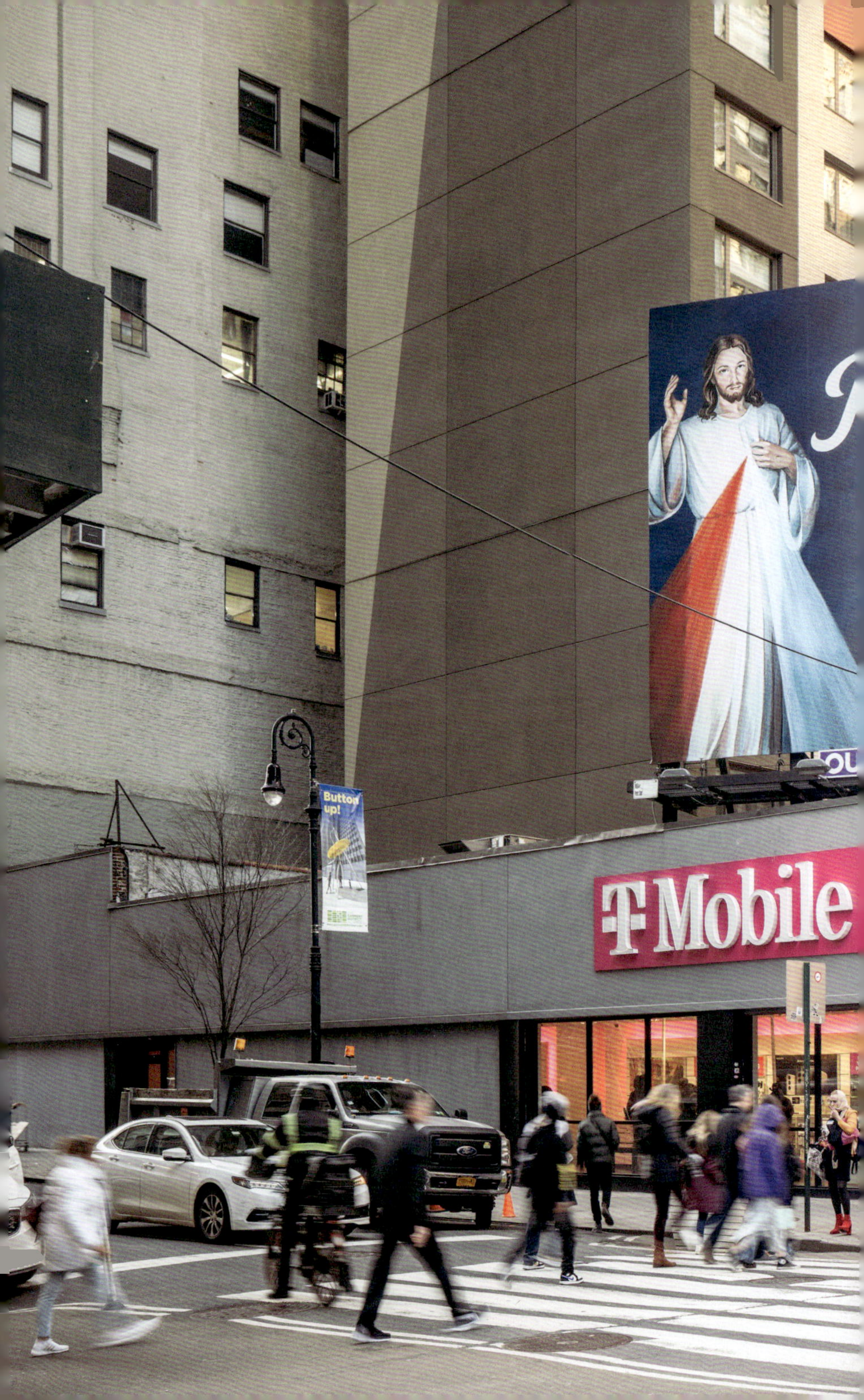
Button up!
T Mobile

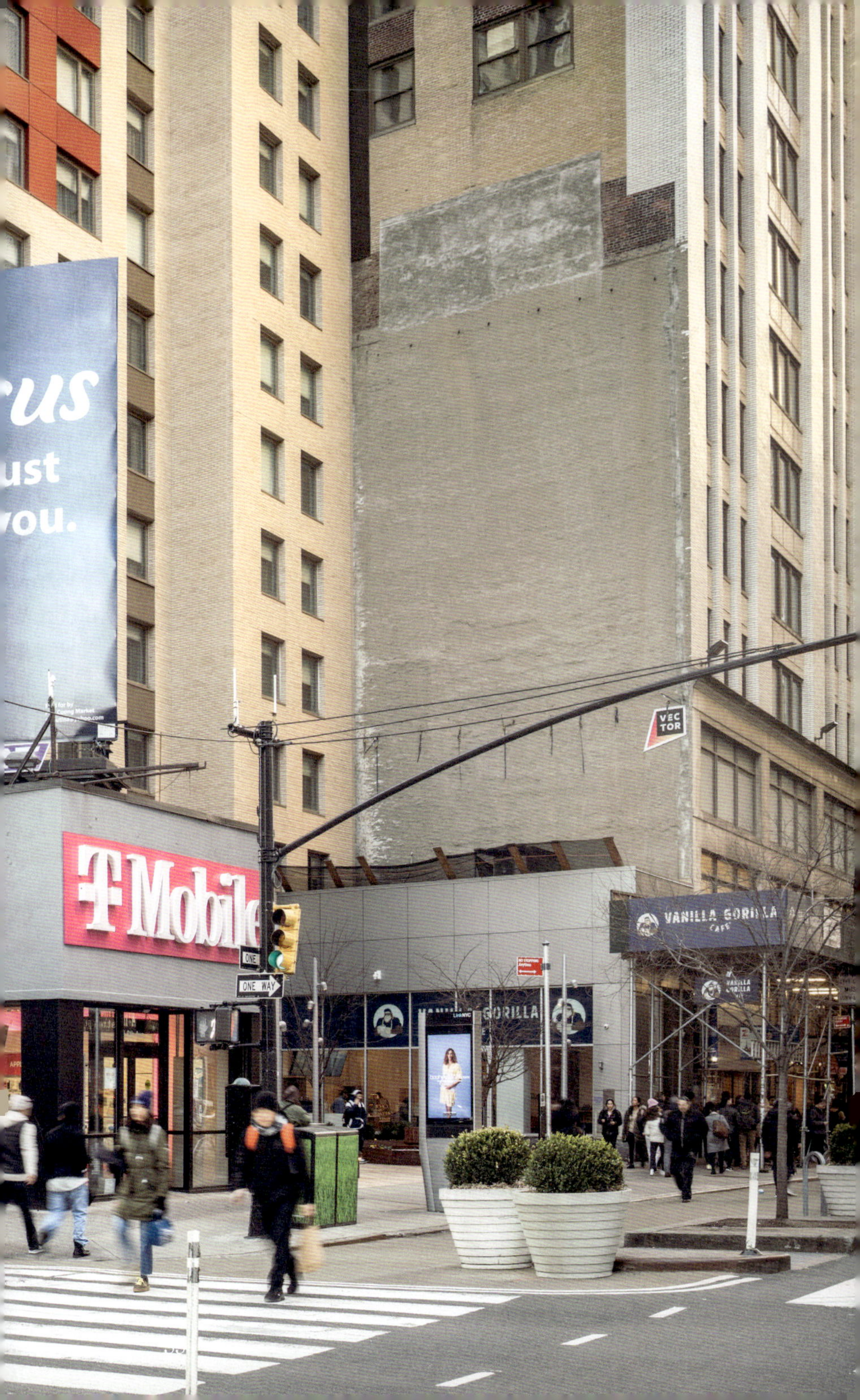
VEC
TOR
T Mobile
ONE WAY
VANILLA GORILLA
CAFE

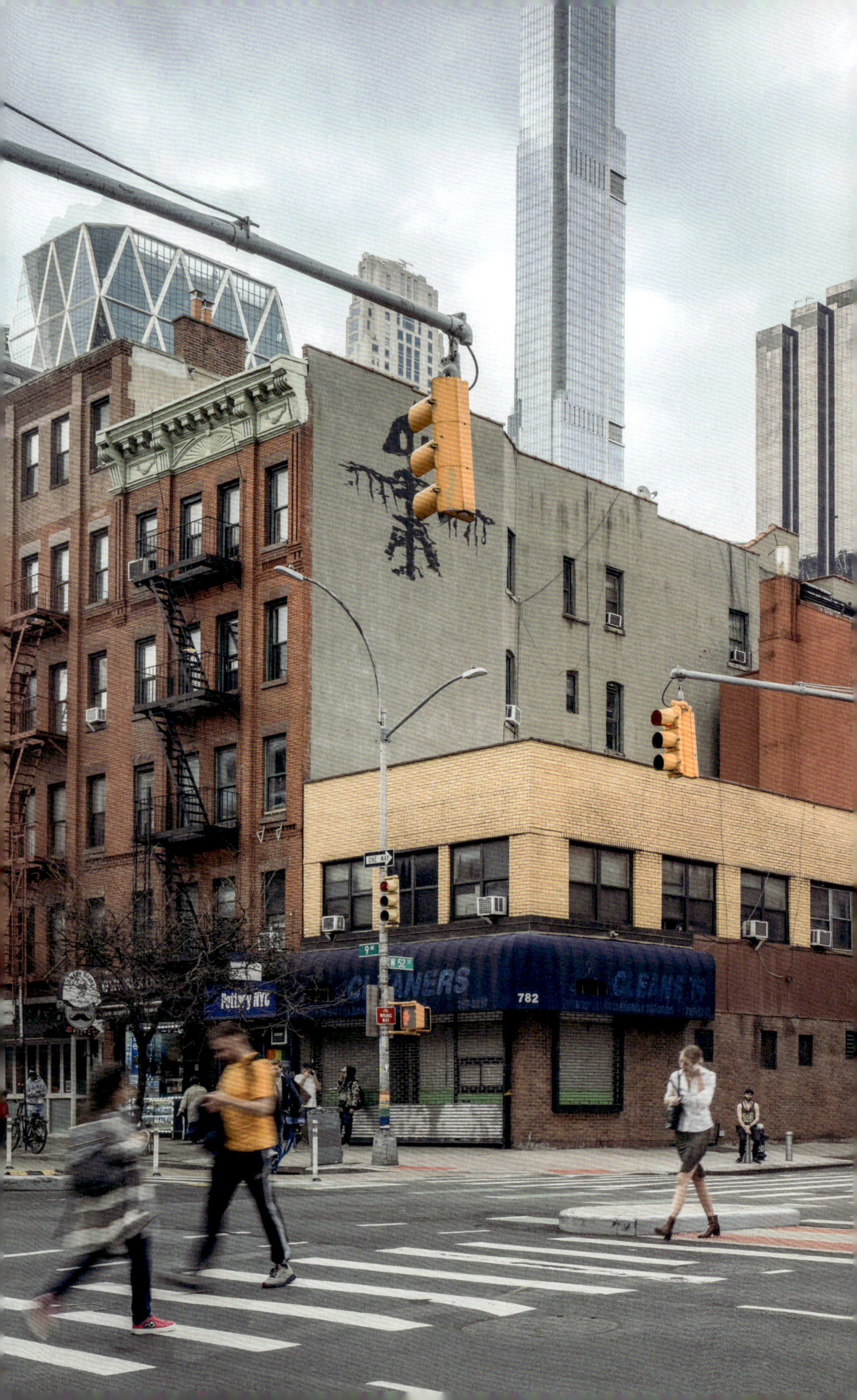
ONE WAY
Pottery NYC
782

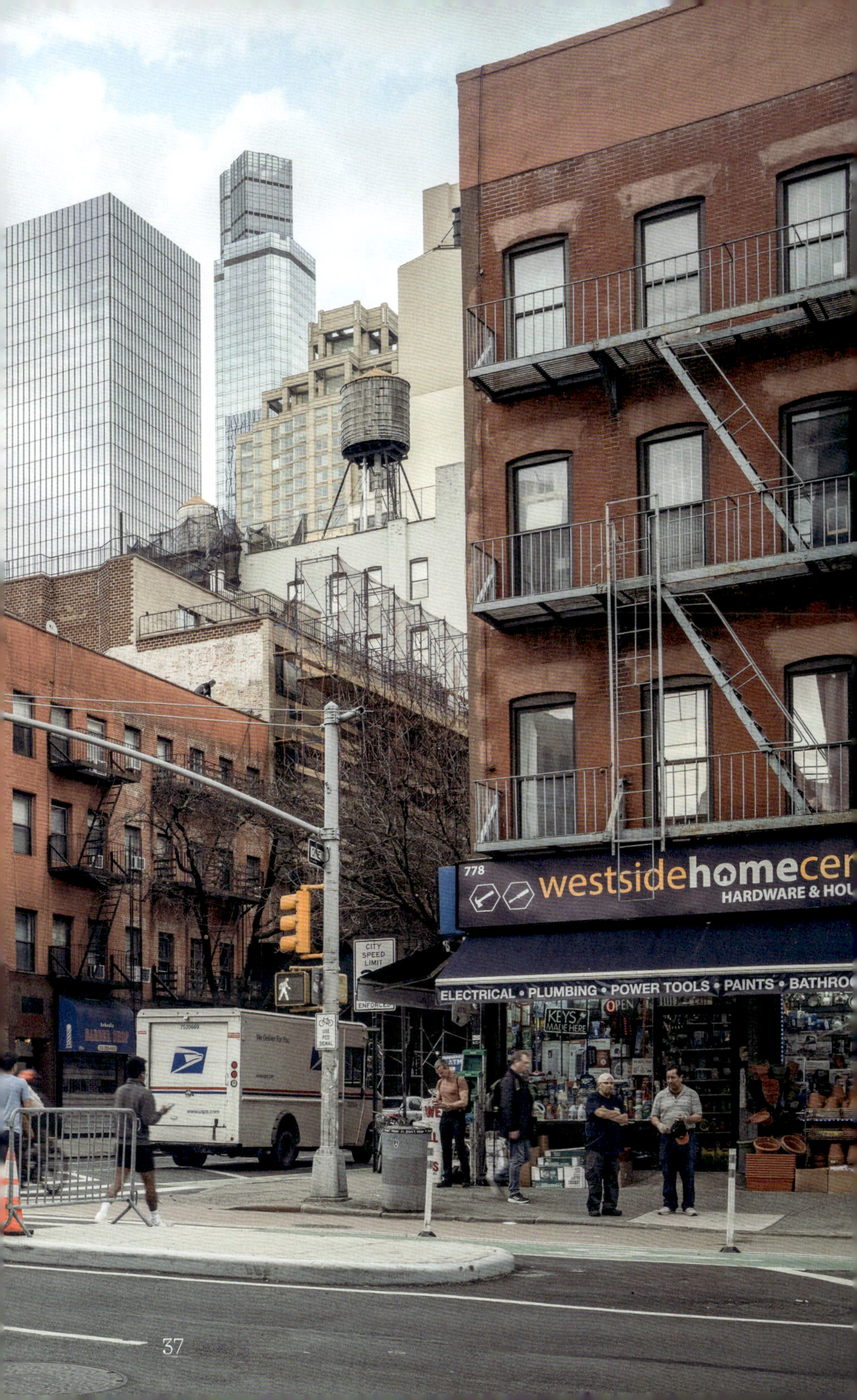
778
ELECTRICAL • PLUMBING • POWER TOOLS • PAINTS •
KEYS MADE HERE
OPEN
CITY SPEED LIMIT
ENFORCED

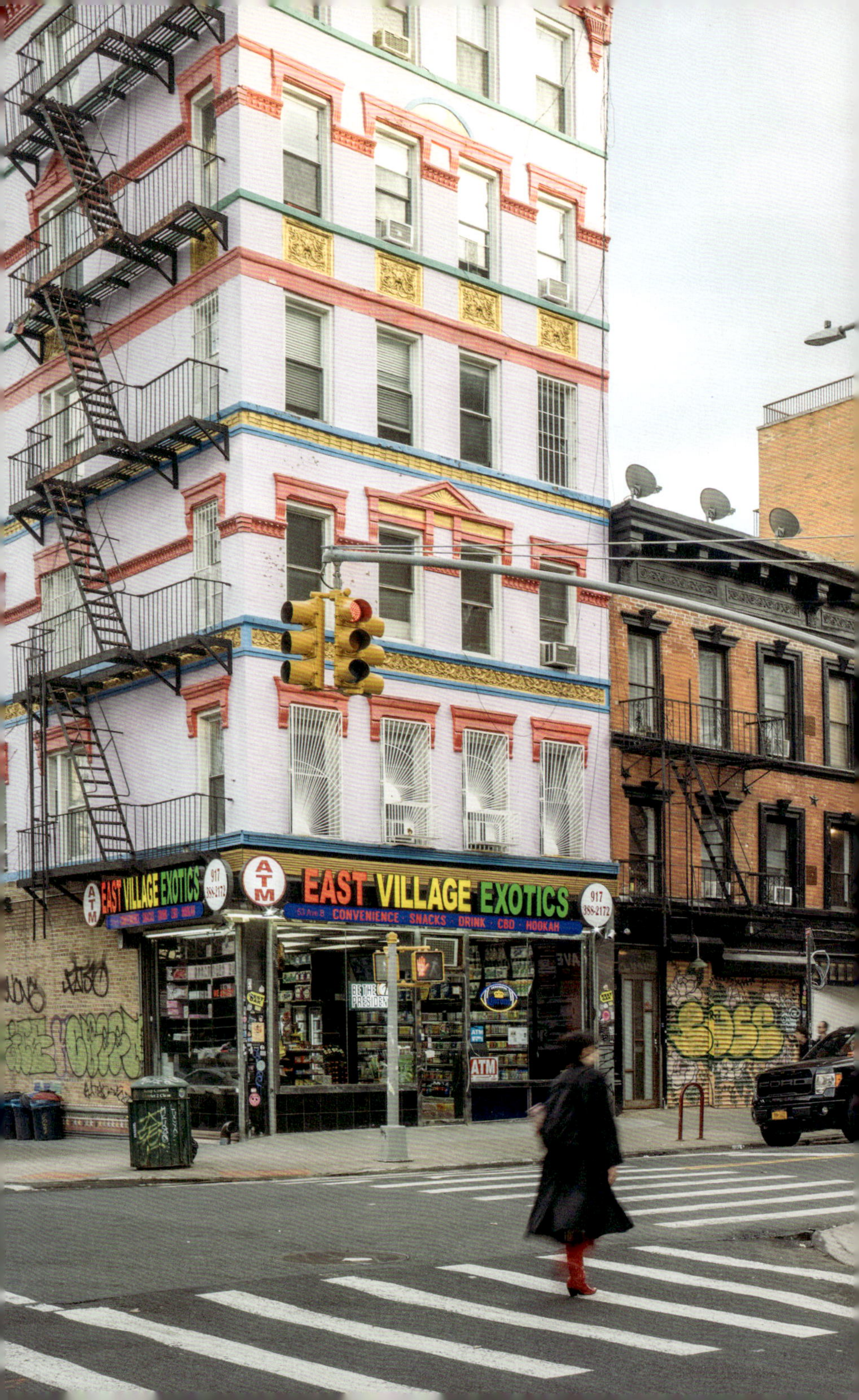
EAST VILLAGE EXOTICS
917
388-2172
ATM
53 Ave B CONVENIENCE · SNACKS · DRINK · CBD · HOOKAH

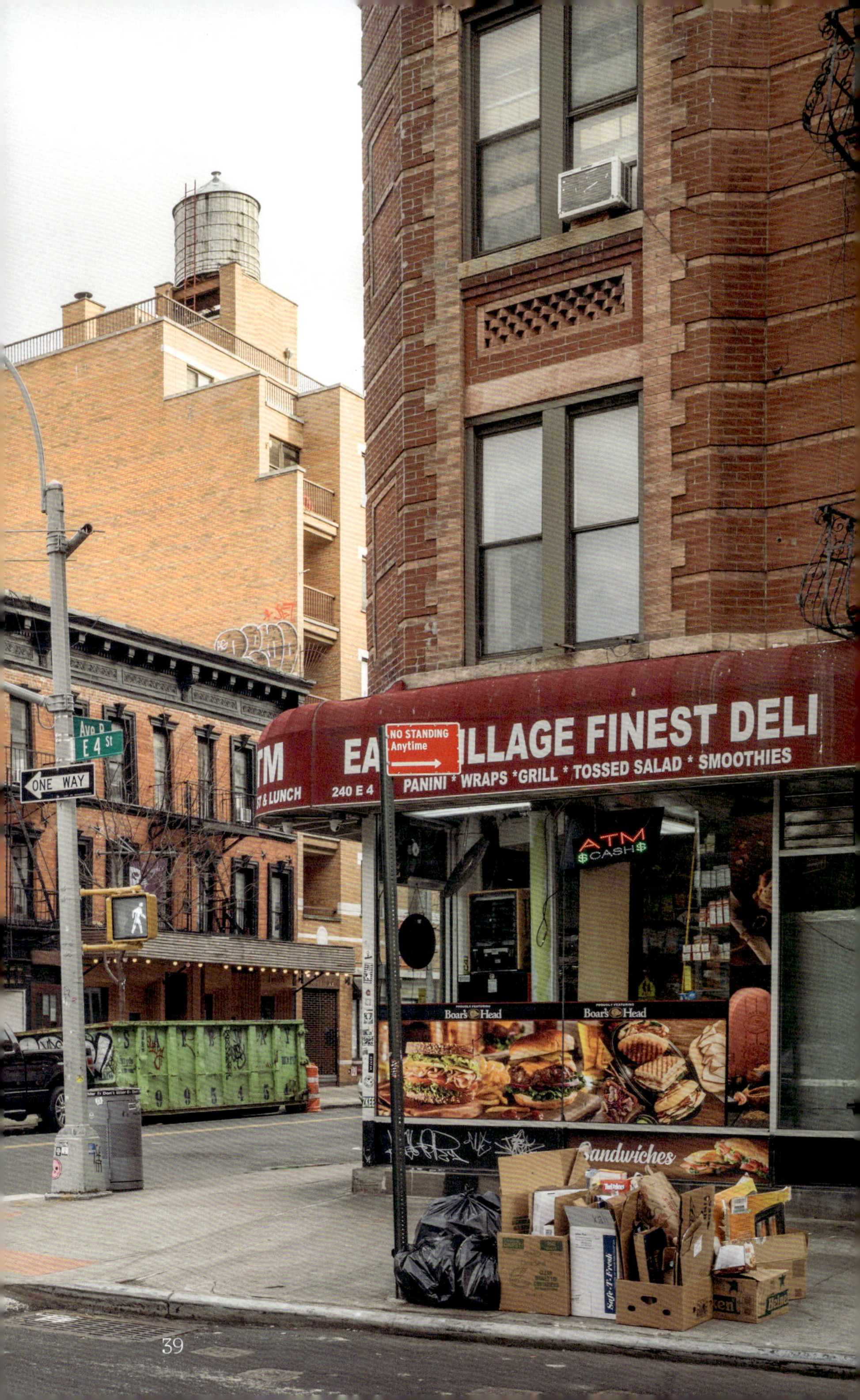

TM
T & LUNCH
EA ILLAGE FINEST DELI
NO STANDING
Anytime
240 E 4
PANINI * WRAPS *GRILL * TOSSED SALAD * SMOOTHIES
ATM
$CASH$
Boar's Head
Boar's Head
Sandwiches
Ave B
E 4 St
ONE WAY

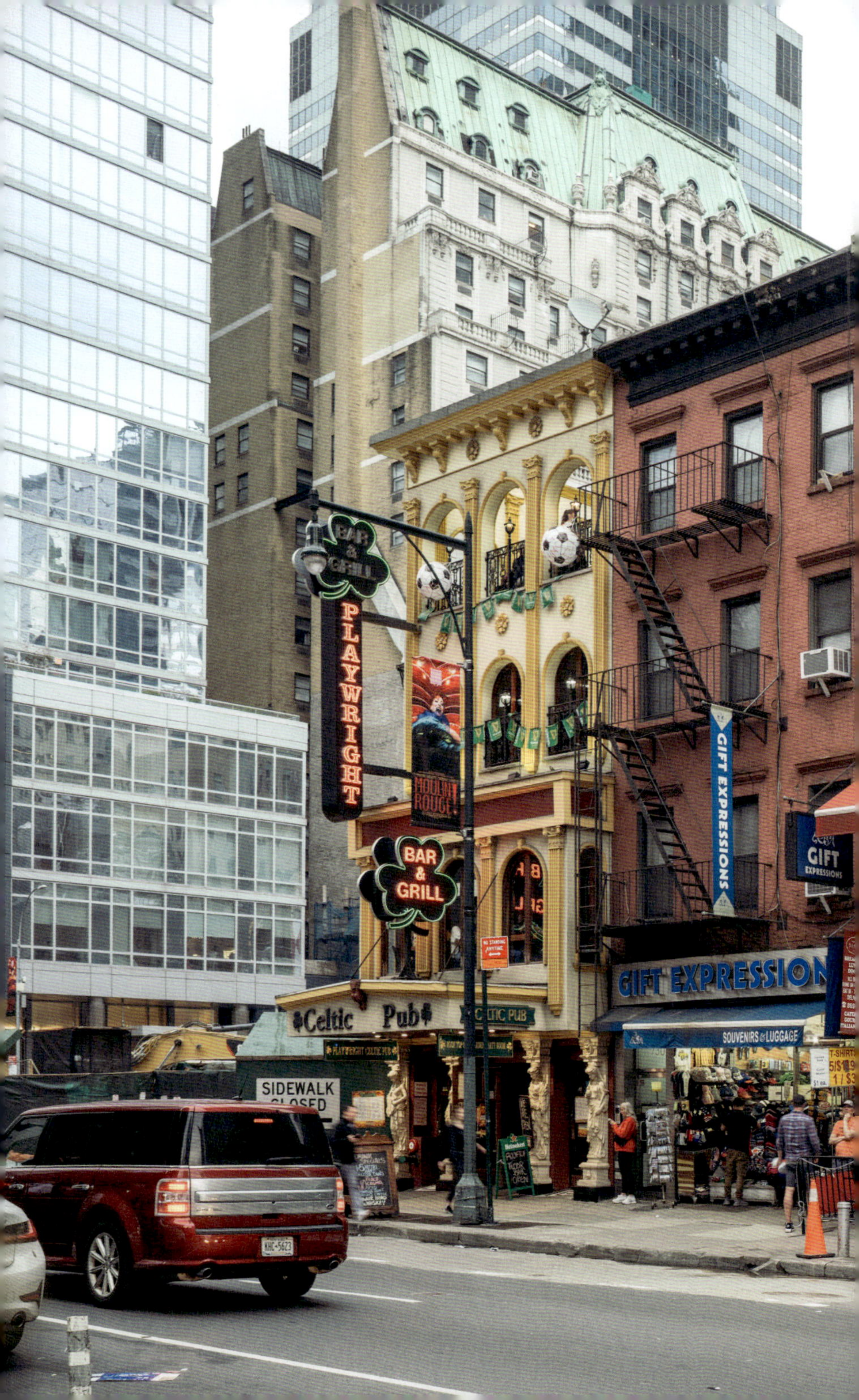
BAR & GRILL
PLAYWRIGHT
MOULIN ROUGE!
BAR & GRILL
GIFT EXPRESSIONS
GIFT EXPRESSIONS
GIFT EXPRESSION
Celtic Pub
CELTIC PUB
SOUVENIRS & LUGGAGE
SIDEWALK CLOSED

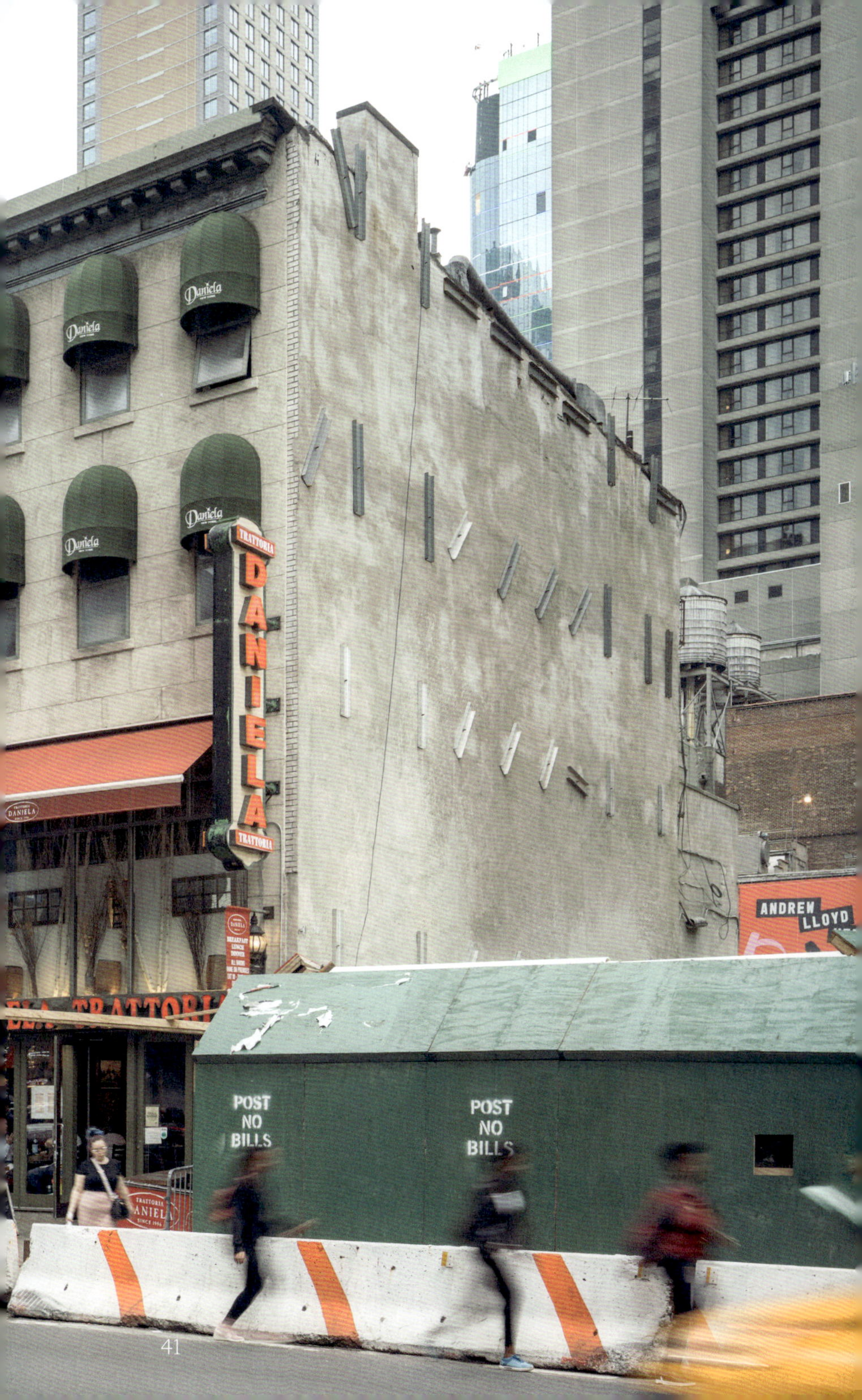
Daniela
TRATTORIA
DANIELA
TRATTORIA
POST
NO
BILLS
POST
NO
BILLS
ANDREW
LLOYD

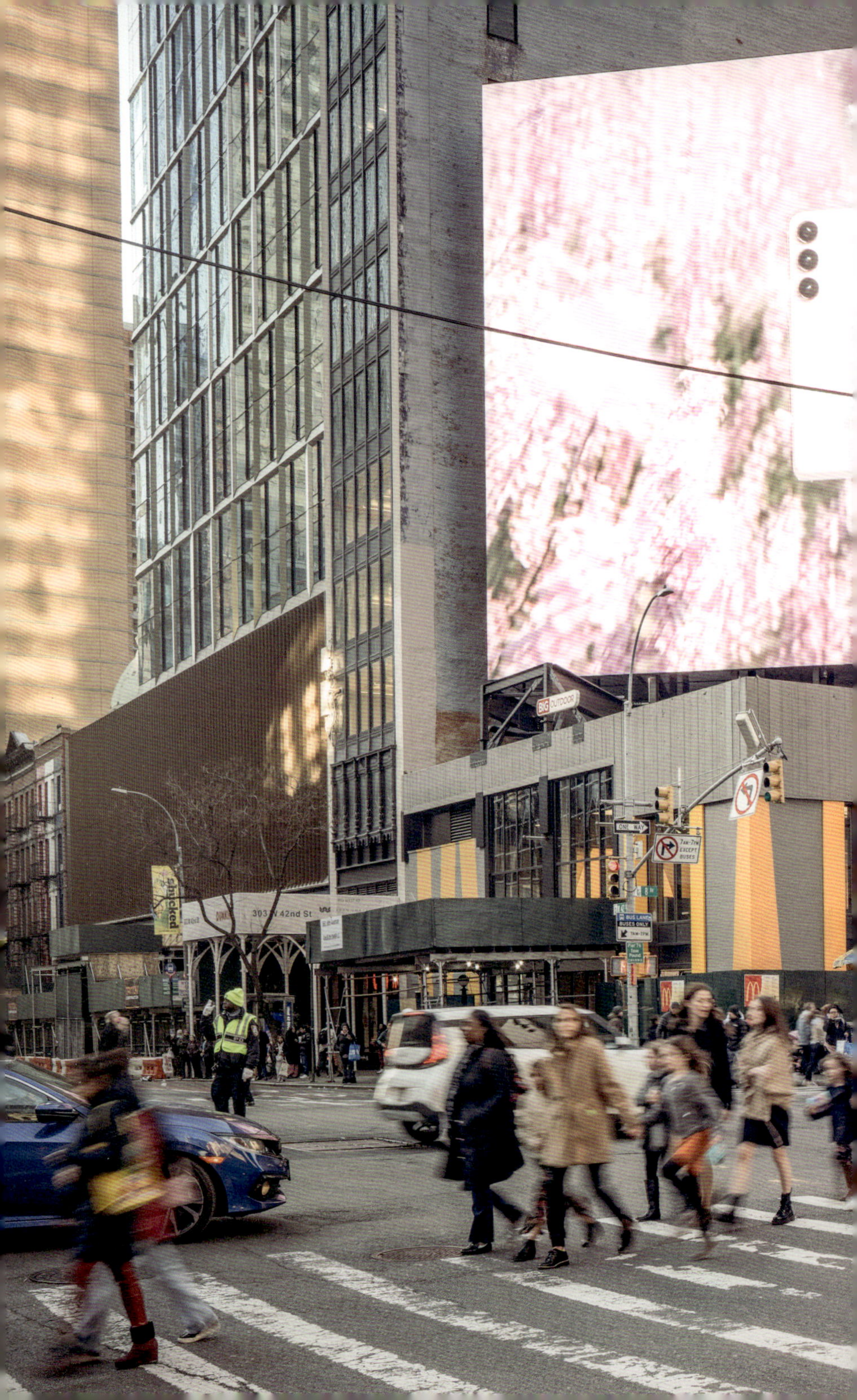

BIG OUTDOOR
ONE WAY
303 W 42nd St

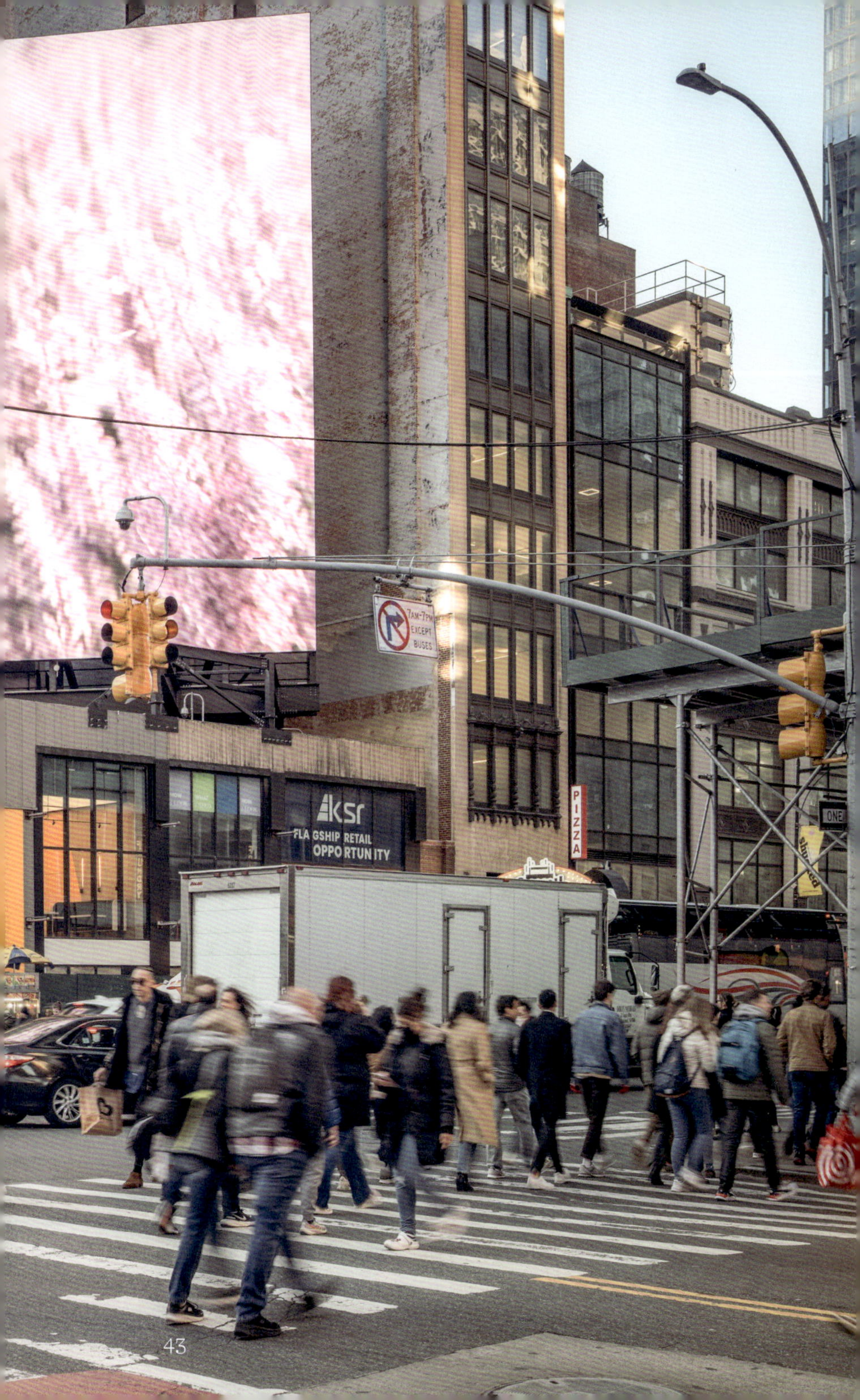
7AM-7PM
EXCEPT
BUSES
ksr
FLAGSHIP RETAIL
OPPORTUNITY
PIZZA
ONE

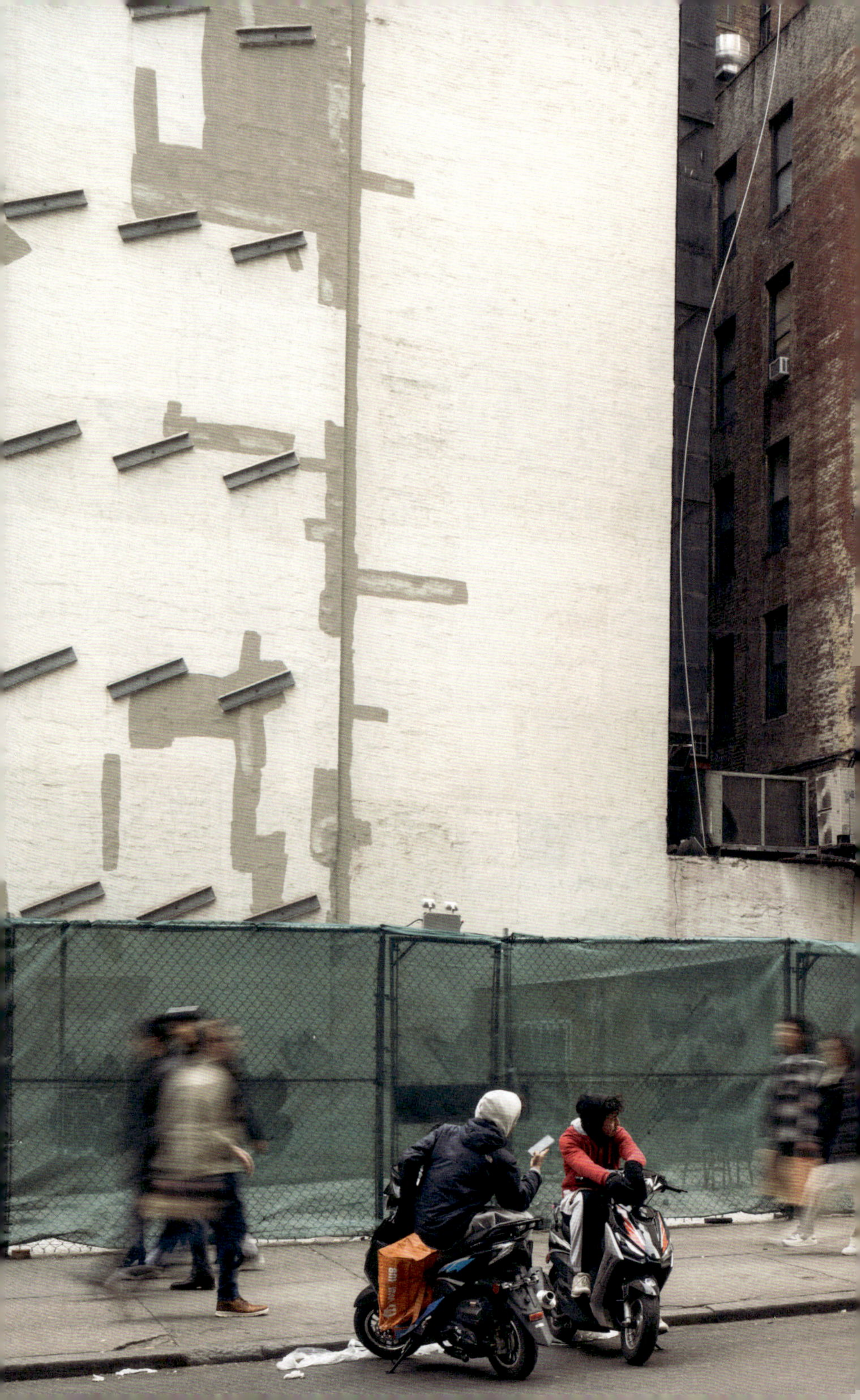

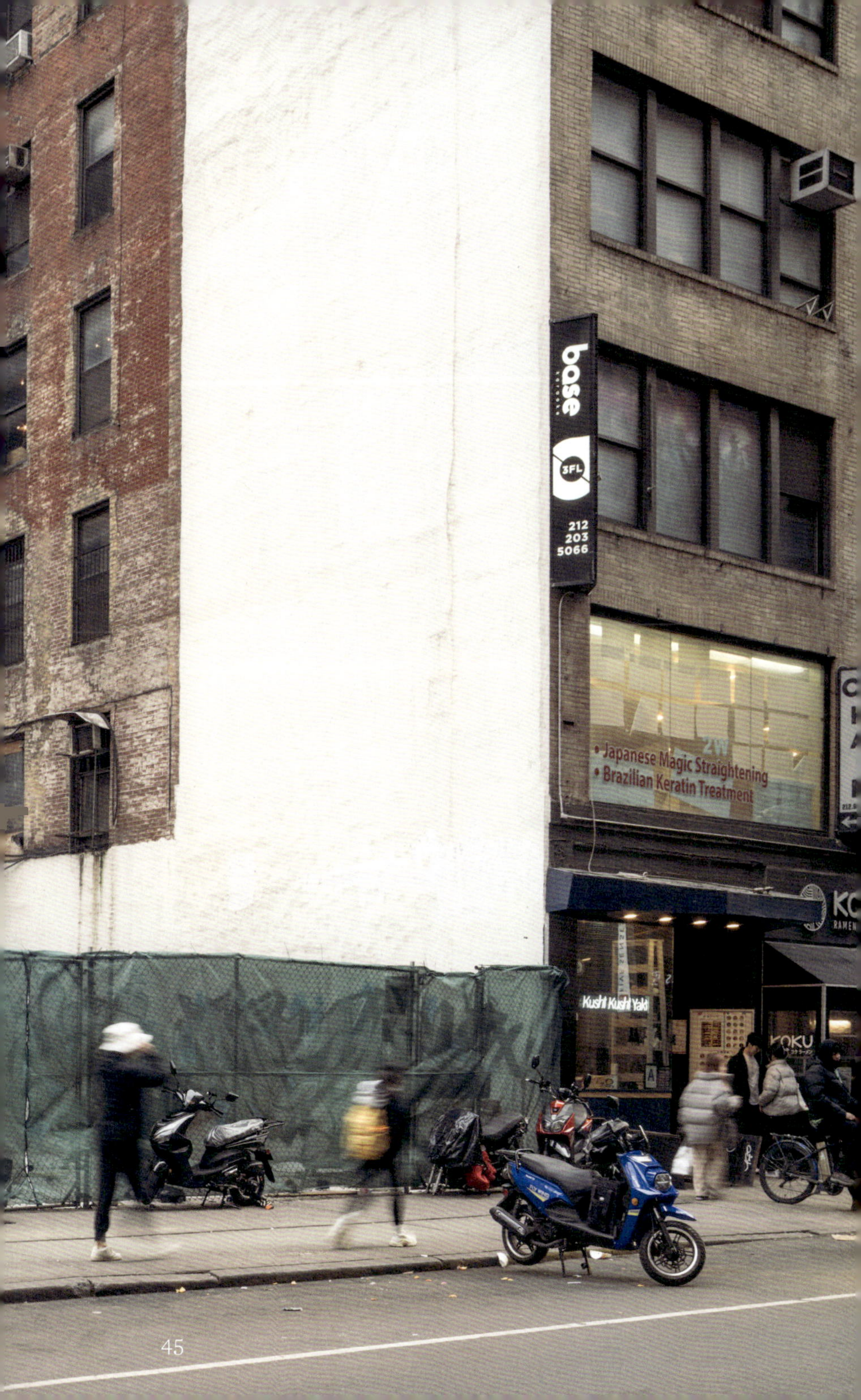
base
3FL
212
203
5066
2W
• Japanese Magic Straightening
• Brazilian Keratin Treatment
Kushi Kushi Yaki
KOKU

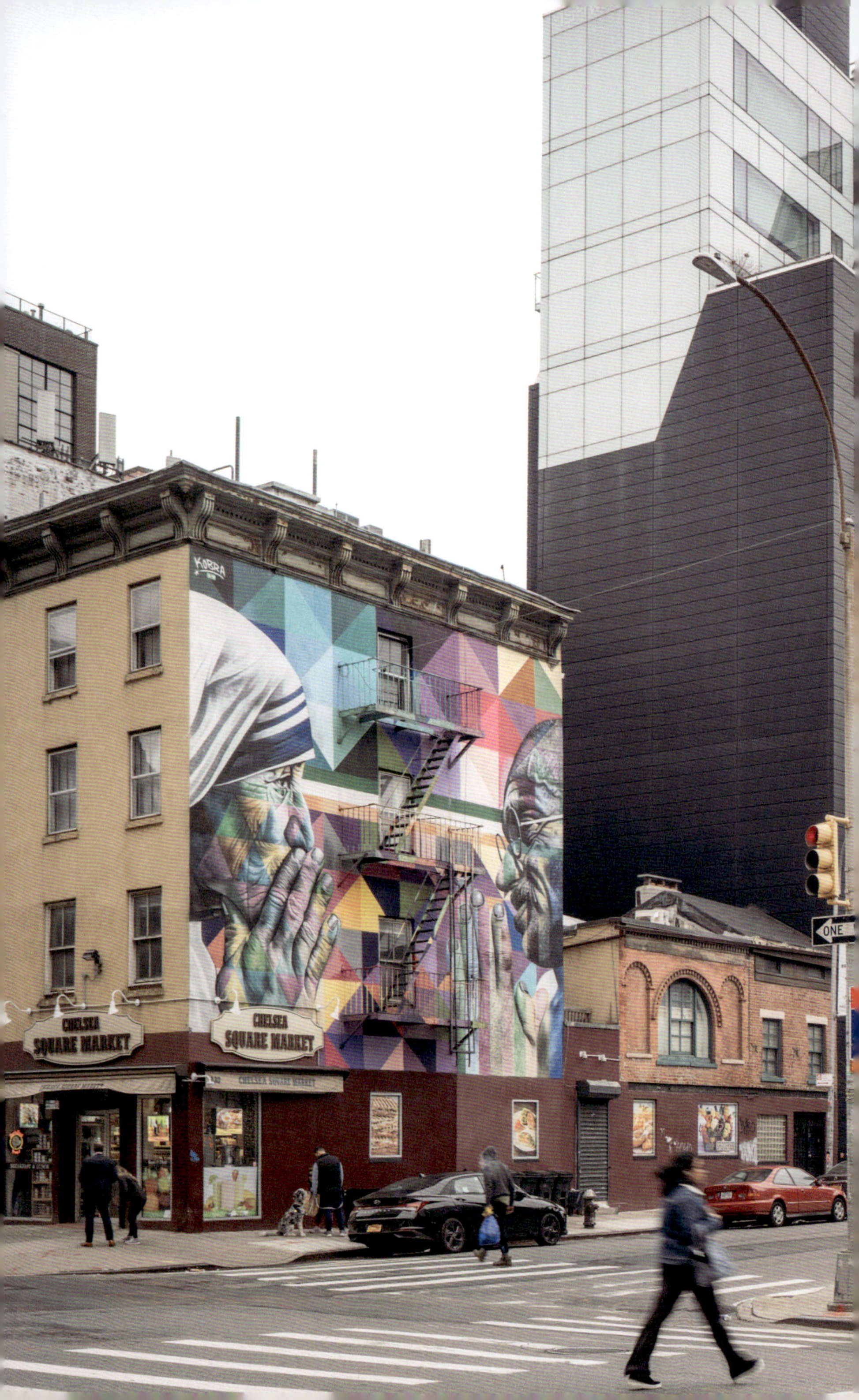
KOBRA
CHELSEA SQUARE MARKET
CHELSEA SQUARE MARKET
CHELSEA SQUARE MARKET
ONE

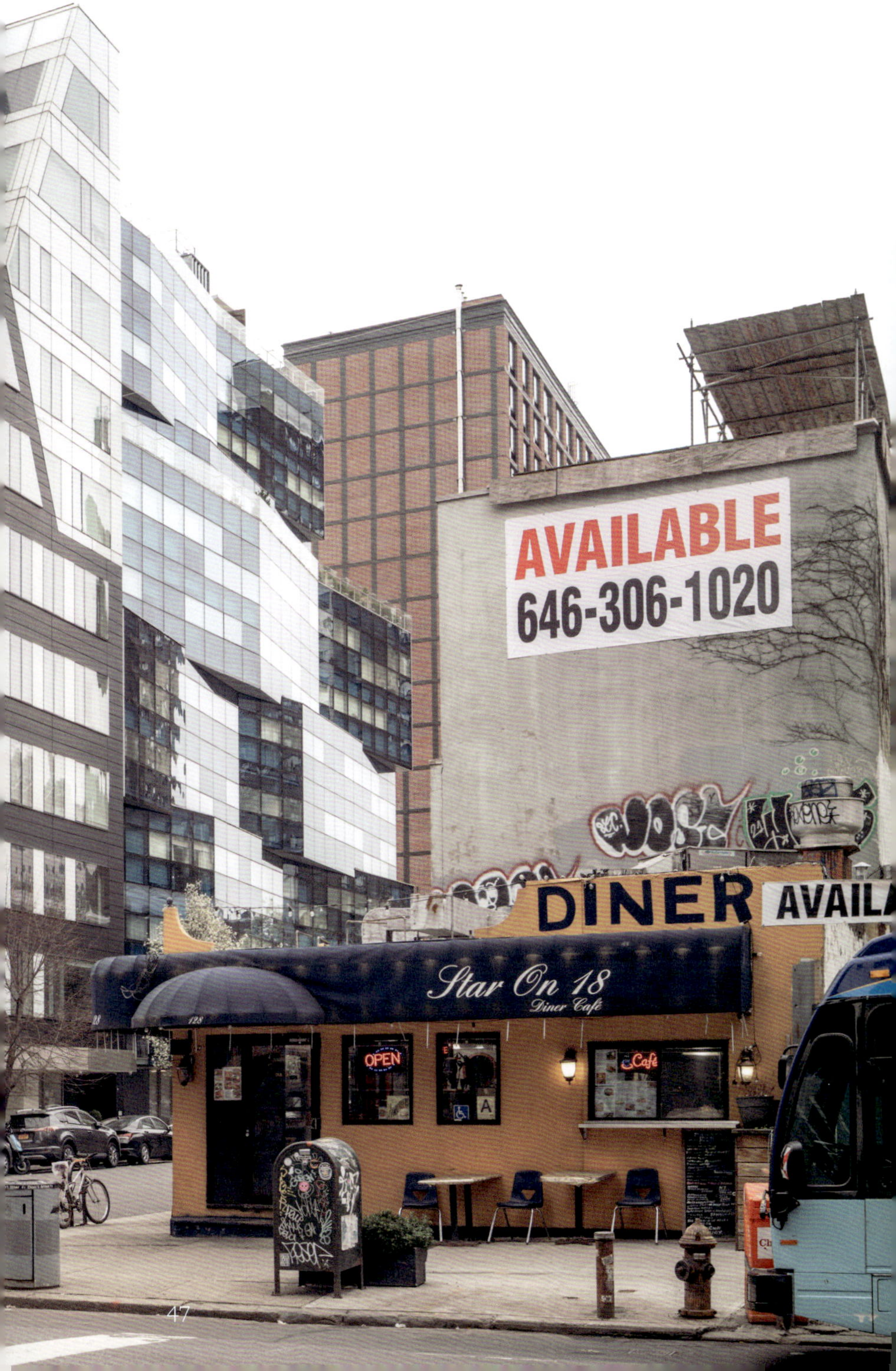
AVAILABLE
646-306-1020
DINER
Star On 18
Diner Café
OPEN
Café

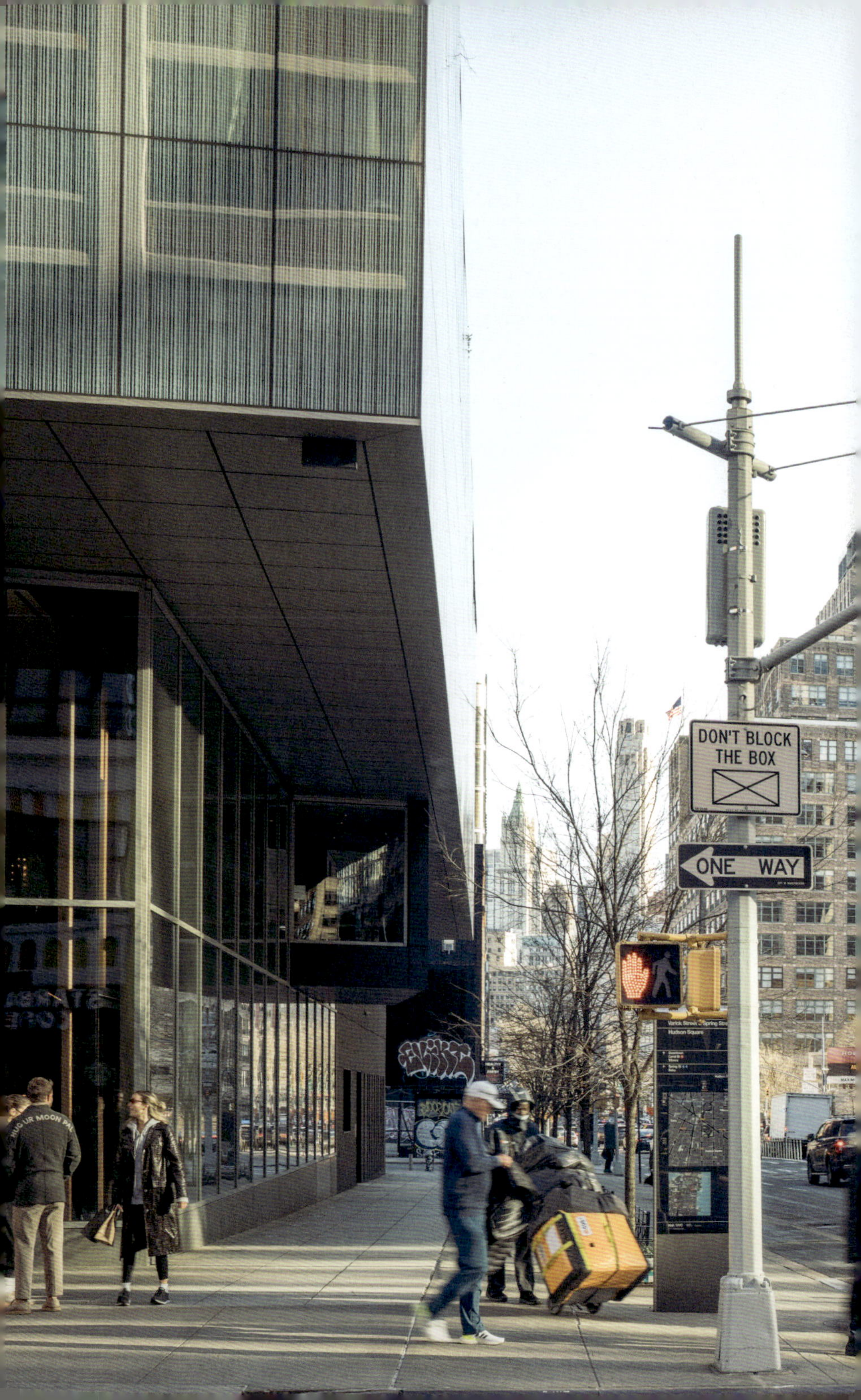
DON'T BLOCK
THE BOX
ONE WAY

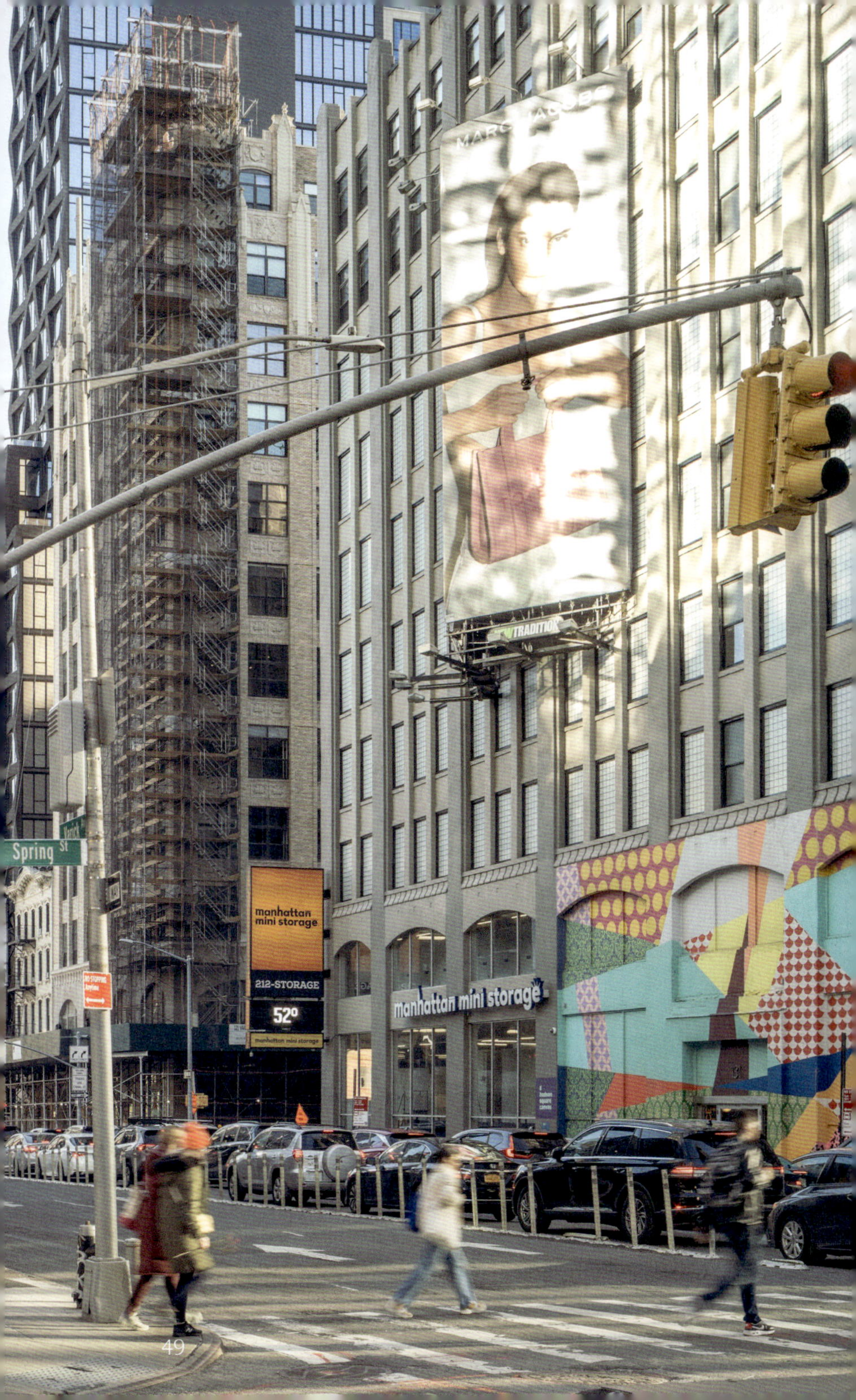
Spring St
manhattan mini storage
212-STORAGE
52°
manhattan mini storage

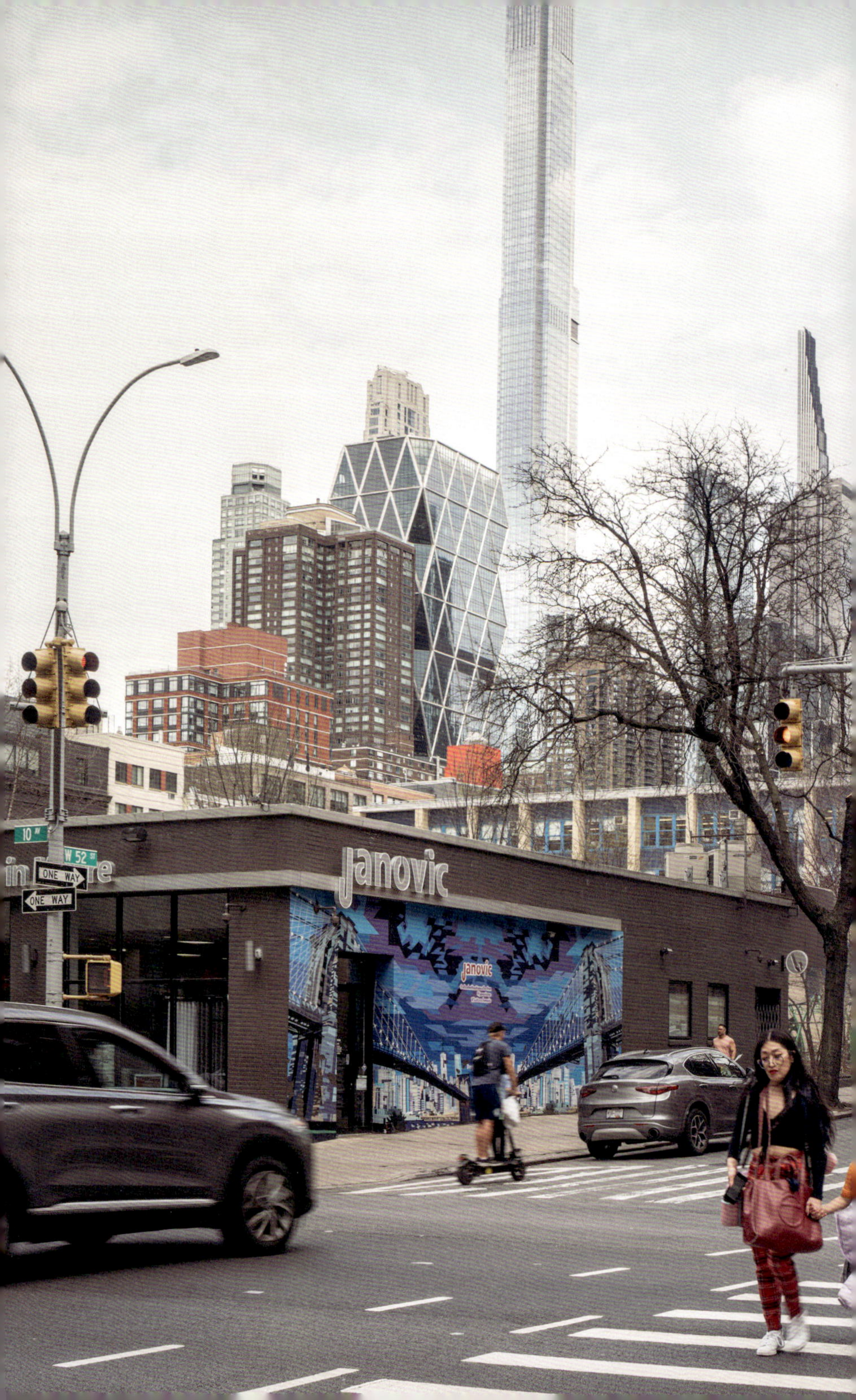
10 AV
W 52 ST
ONE WAY
ONE WAY
janovic
janovic

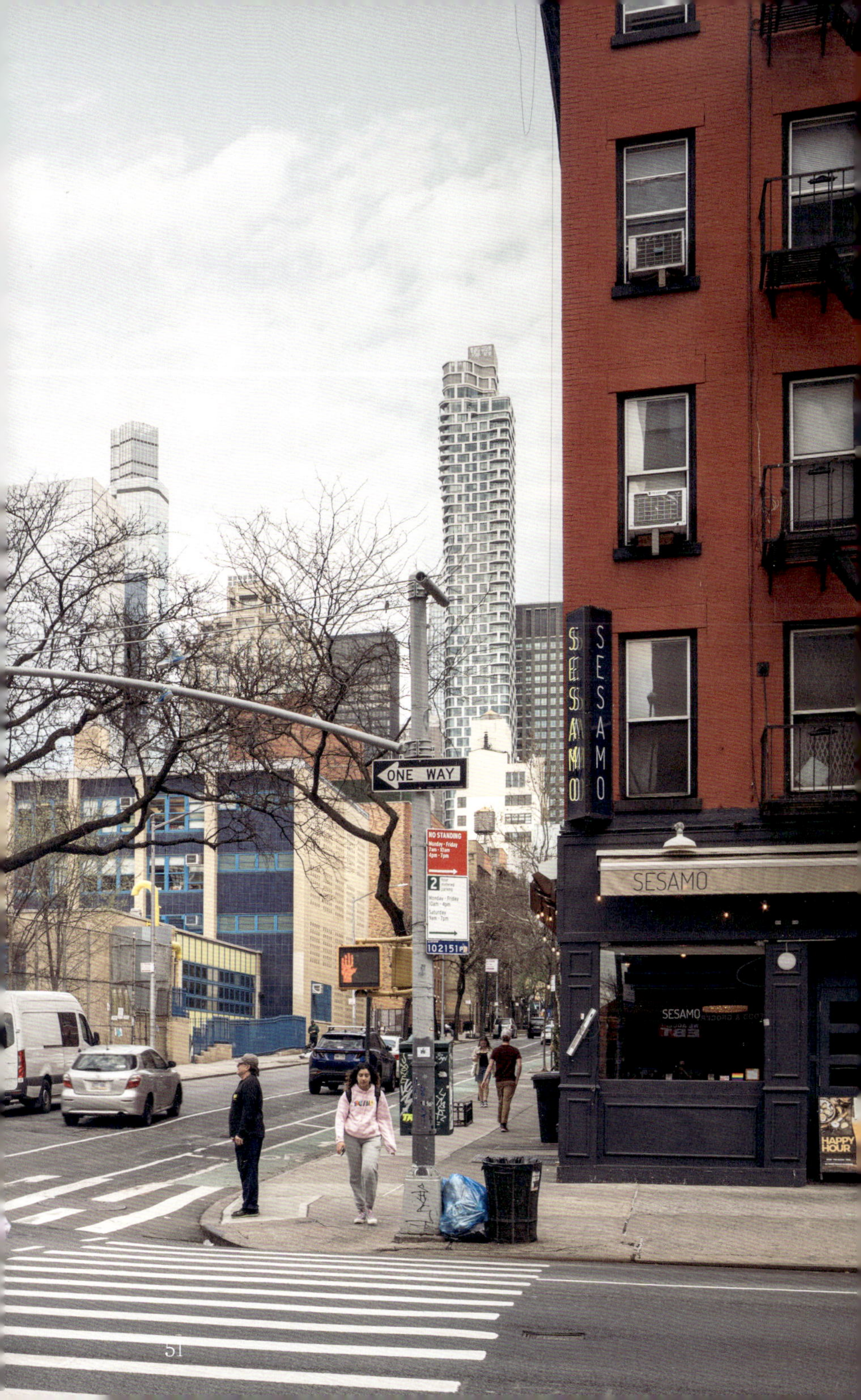
ONE WAY
SESAMO
SESAMO
SESAMO
NO STANDING
HAPPY HOUR

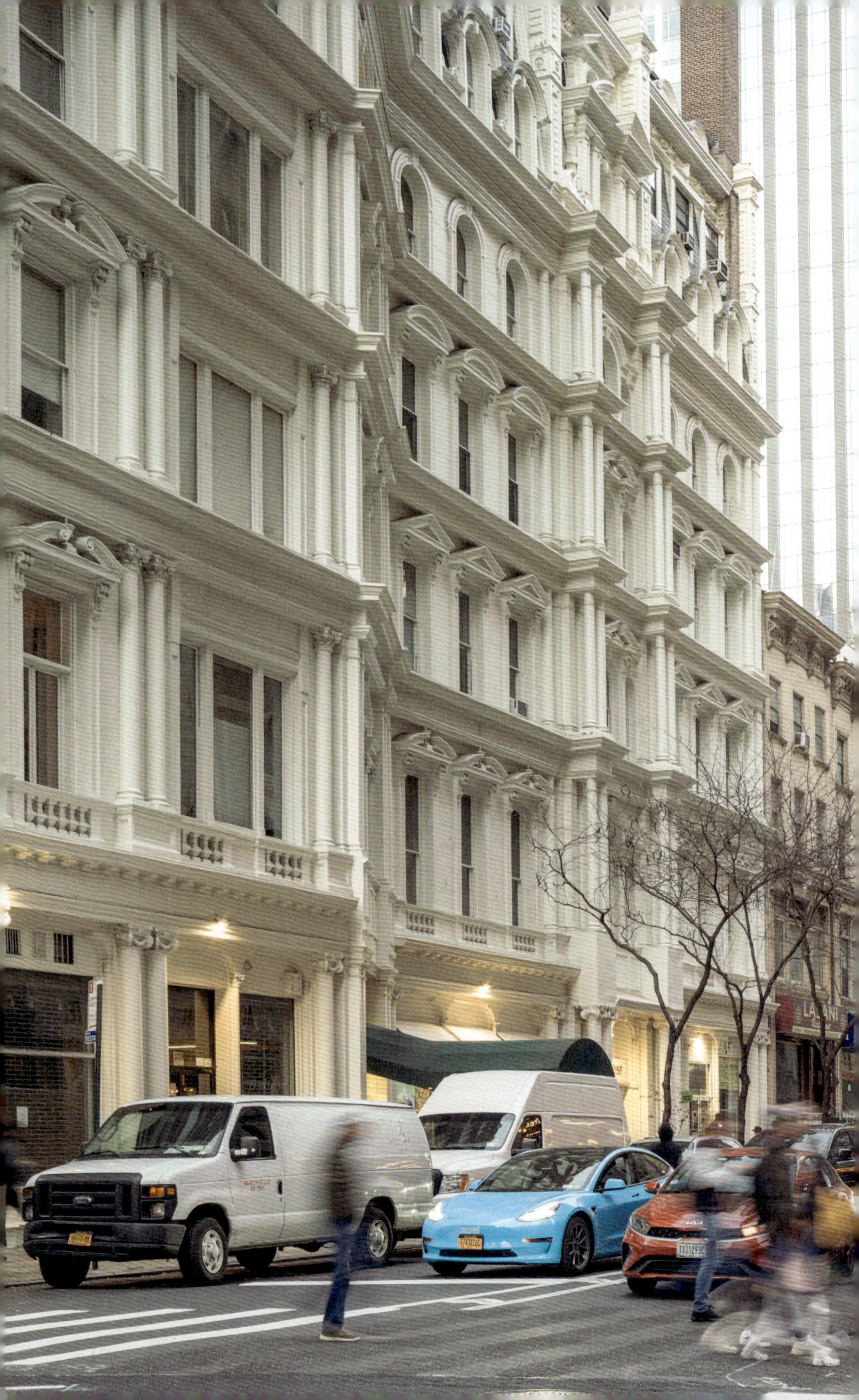

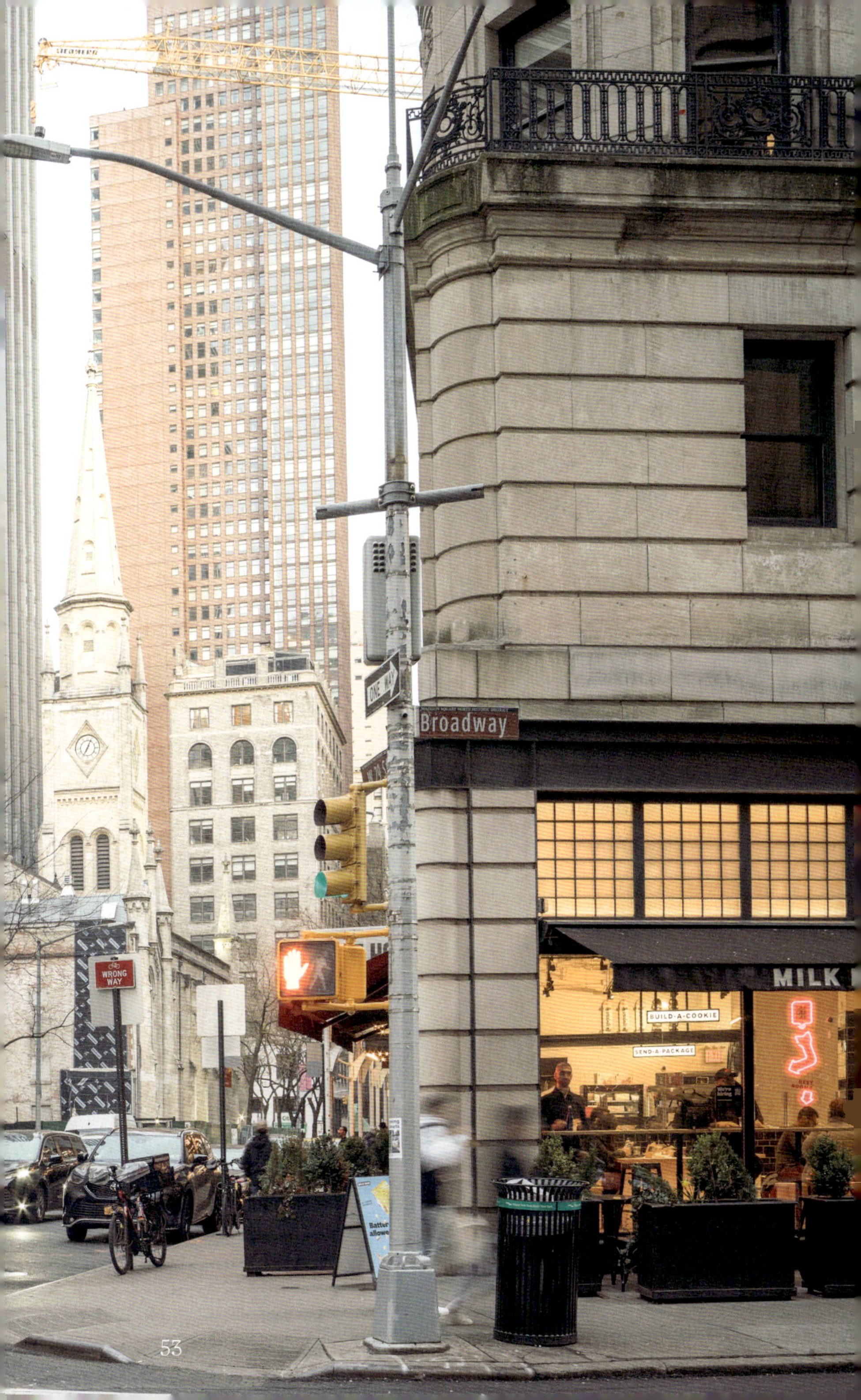
Broadway
ONE WAY
WRONG WAY
MILK
BUILD-A-COOKIE
SEND-A-PACKAGE

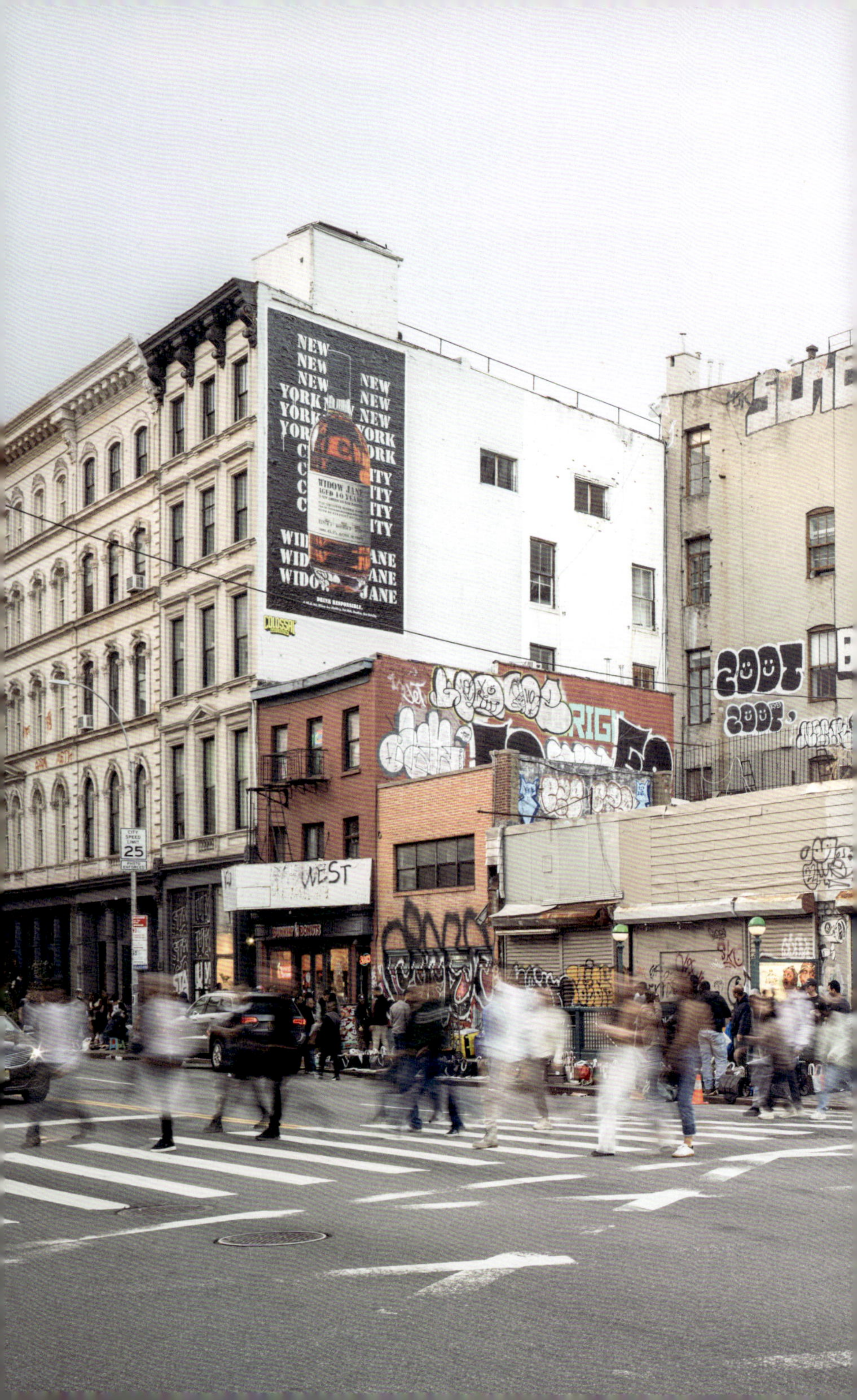
NEW
NEW
NEW
YORK
YORK
NEW
NEW
NEW
YORK
WIDOW JANE
JANE
JANE
JANE
DRINK RESPONSIBLY
COLOSSAL
CITY
SPEED
LIMIT
25
WEST

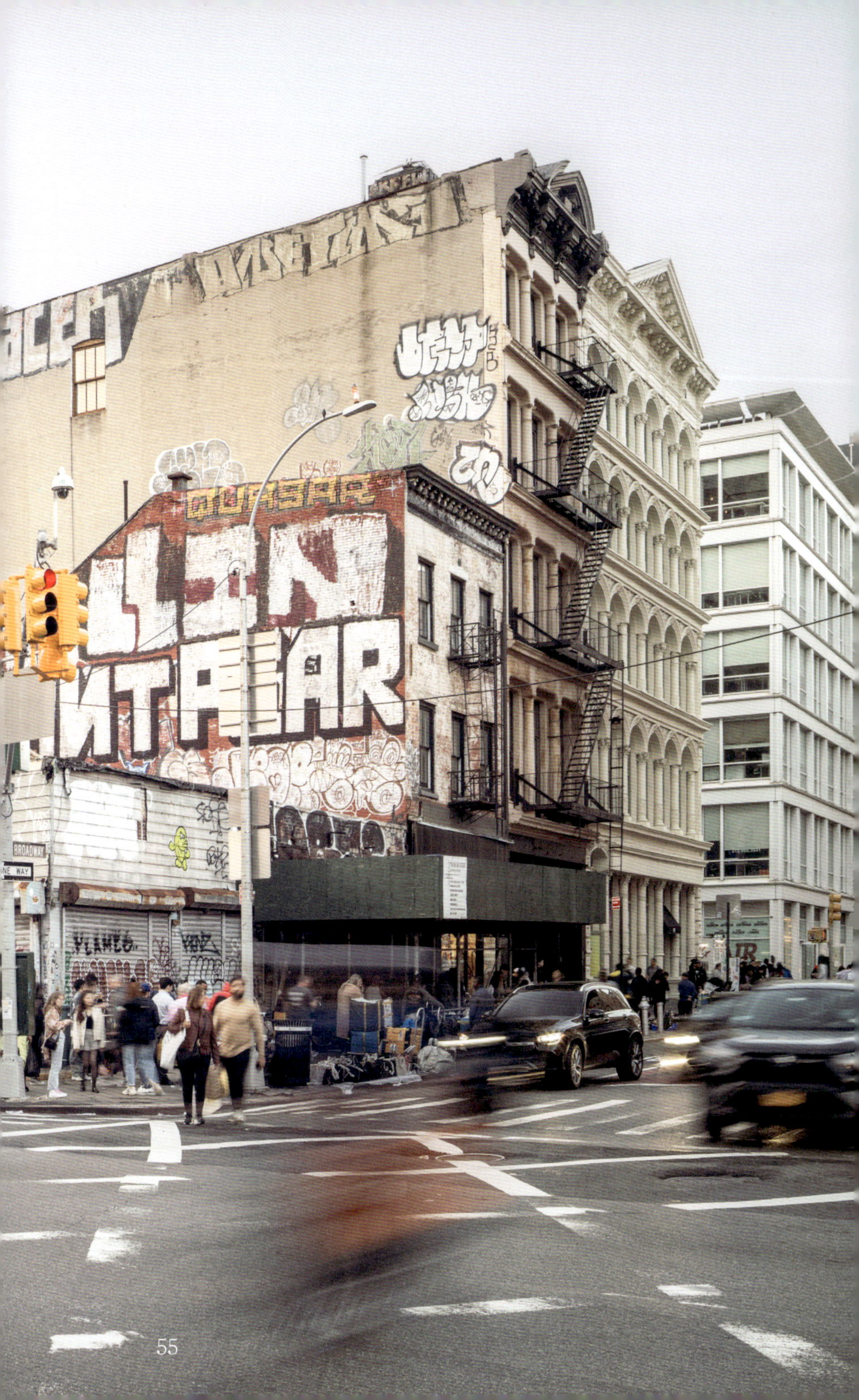
BROADWAY

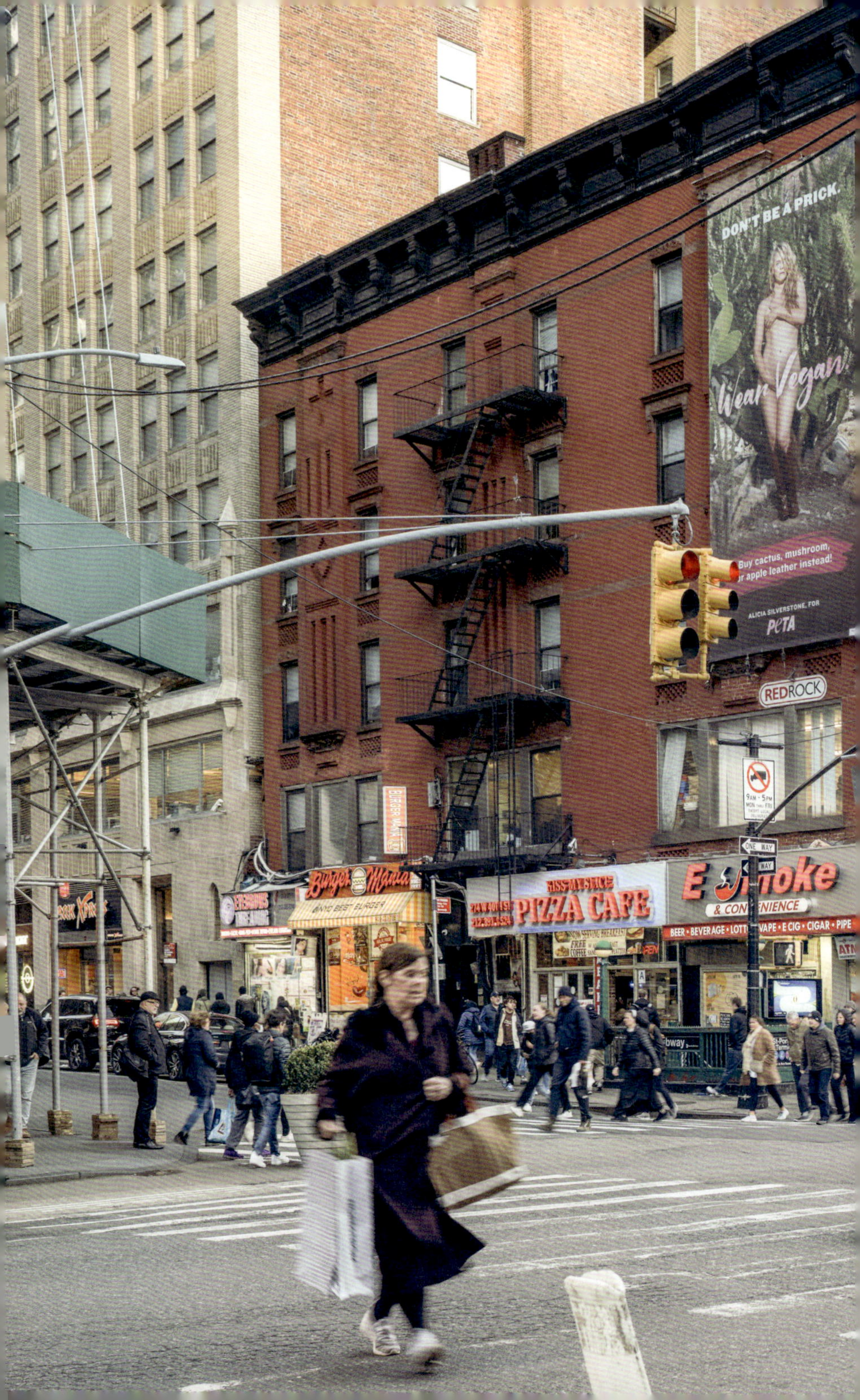

DON'T BE A PRICK.
Wear Vegan.
Buy cactus, mushroom,
ALICIA SILVERSTONE, FOR
PETA
REDROCK
ONE WAY
Burger Mania
NYC BEST BURGER
PIZZA CAFE
& CONVENIENCE
BEER • BEVERAGE • LOTTO • VAPE • E CIG • CIGAR • PIPE

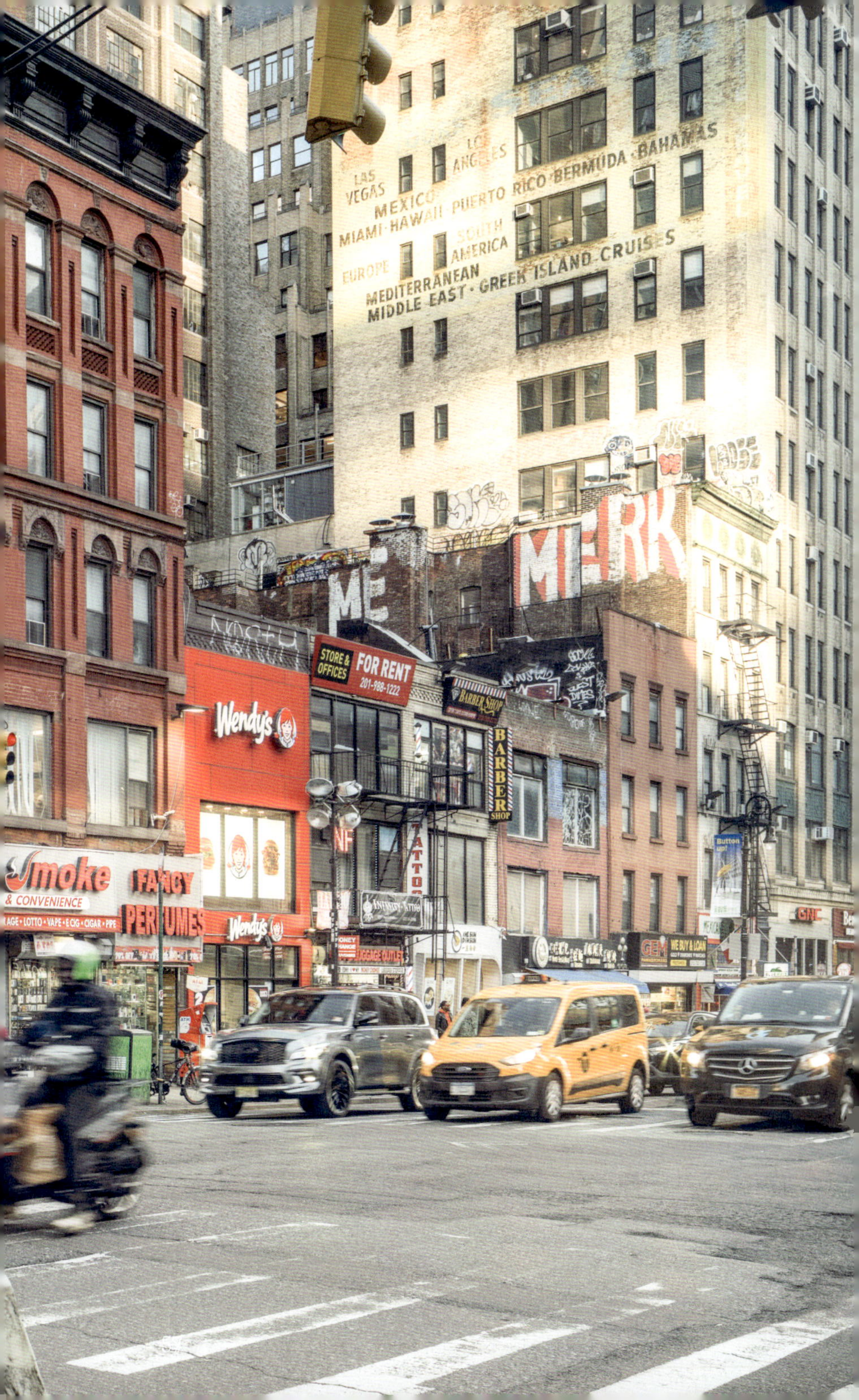
LAS VEGAS
LOS ANGELES
MEXICO
MIAMI · HAWAII · PUERTO RICO · BERMUDA · BAHAMAS
EUROPE
SOUTH AMERICA
MEDITERRANEAN
MIDDLE EAST · GREEK ISLAND CRUISES
STORE & OFFICES
FOR RENT
201-988-1222
BARBER SHOP
Wendy's
Smoke
& CONVENIENCE
FANCY
PERFUMES
Wendy's

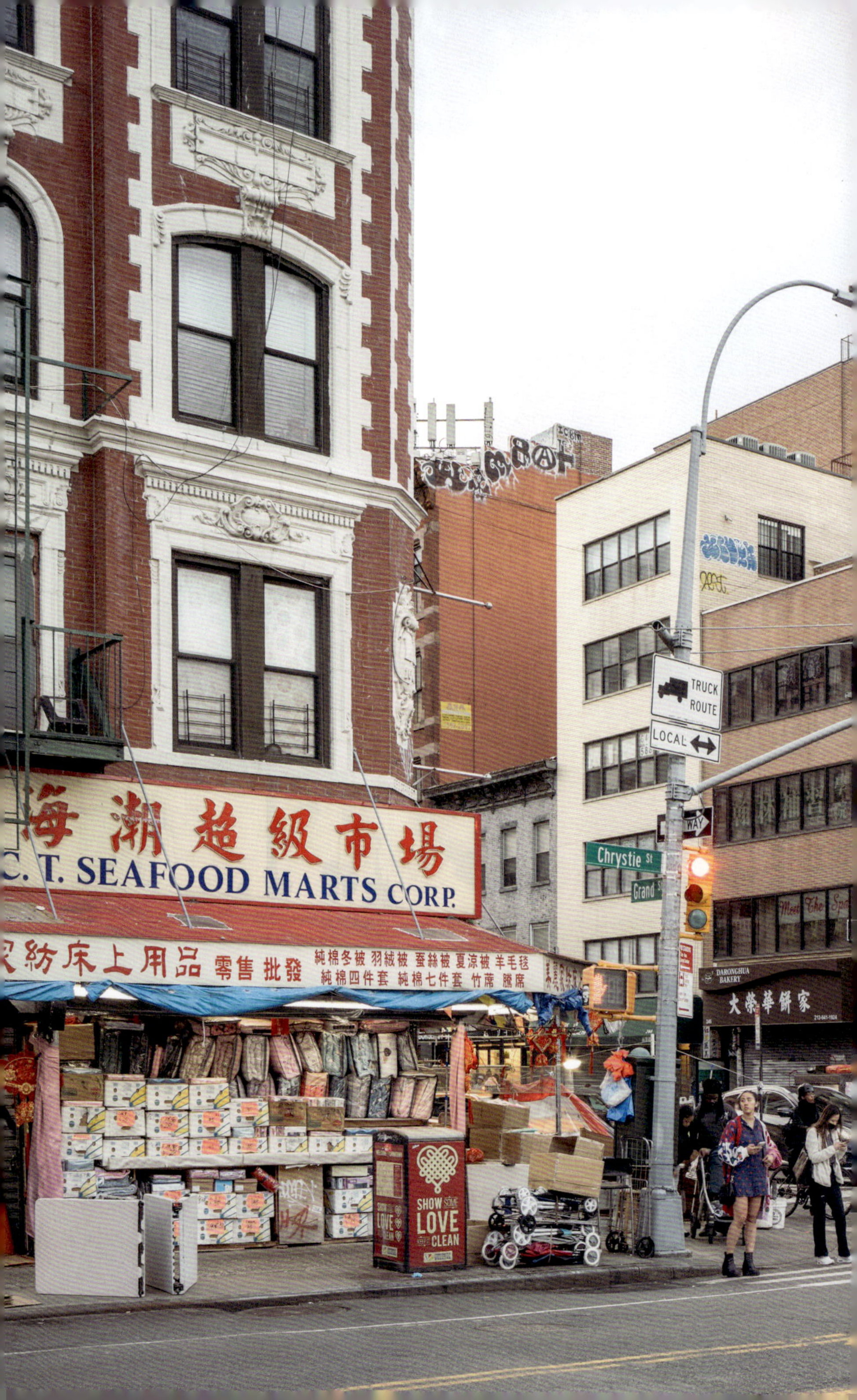
海潮超級市場
C.T. SEAFOOD MARTS CORP.
紡床上用品 零售 批發
純棉冬被 羽絨被 蚕絲被 夏涼被 羊毛毯
純棉四件套 純棉七件套 竹席 籐席
TRUCK ROUTE
LOCAL
Chrystie St
Grand St
DARONGHUA BAKERY
大榮華餅家
SHOW SOME LOVE
CLEAN

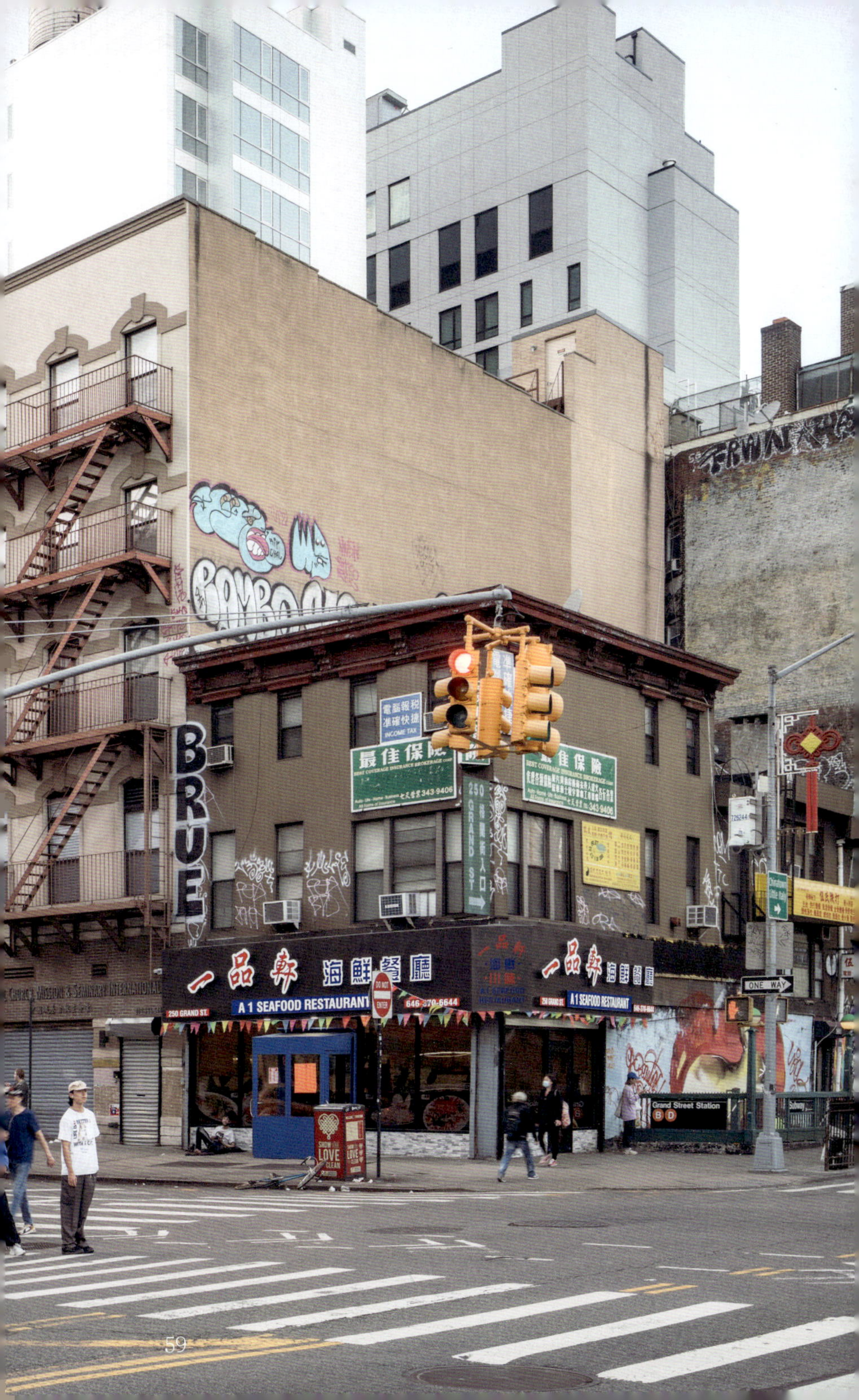

電腦報稅
準確快捷
INCOME TAX
最佳保險
250 GRAND ST
BRUE
海鮮餐廳
A 1 SEAFOOD RESTAURANT
250 GRAND ST.
646-370-6644
DO NOT ENTER
ONE WAY
Grand Street Station

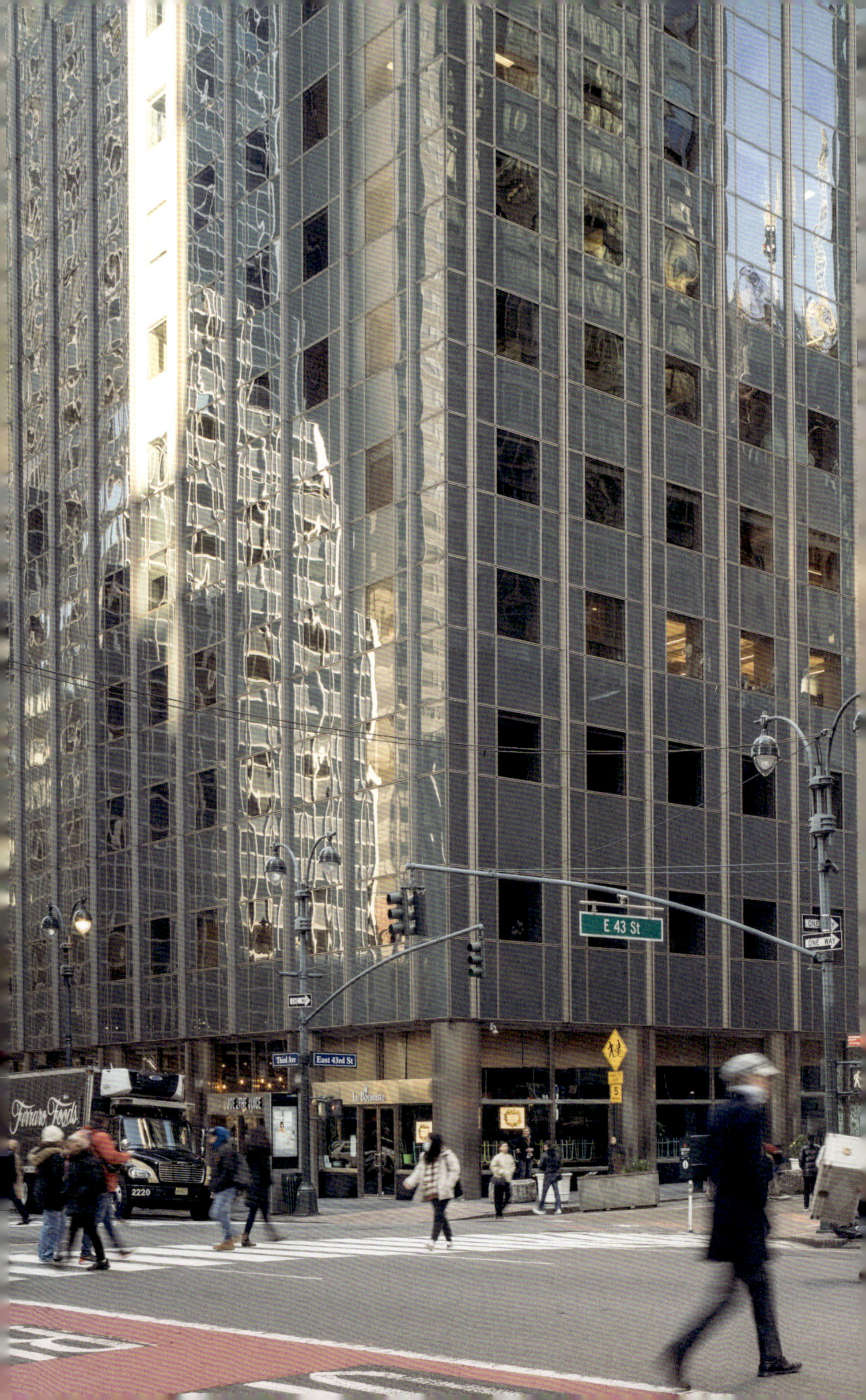

E 43 St
ONE WAY
ONE WAY
Third Ave
East 43rd St
Ferraro Foods
JOE & THE JUICE
Le Bouquiste

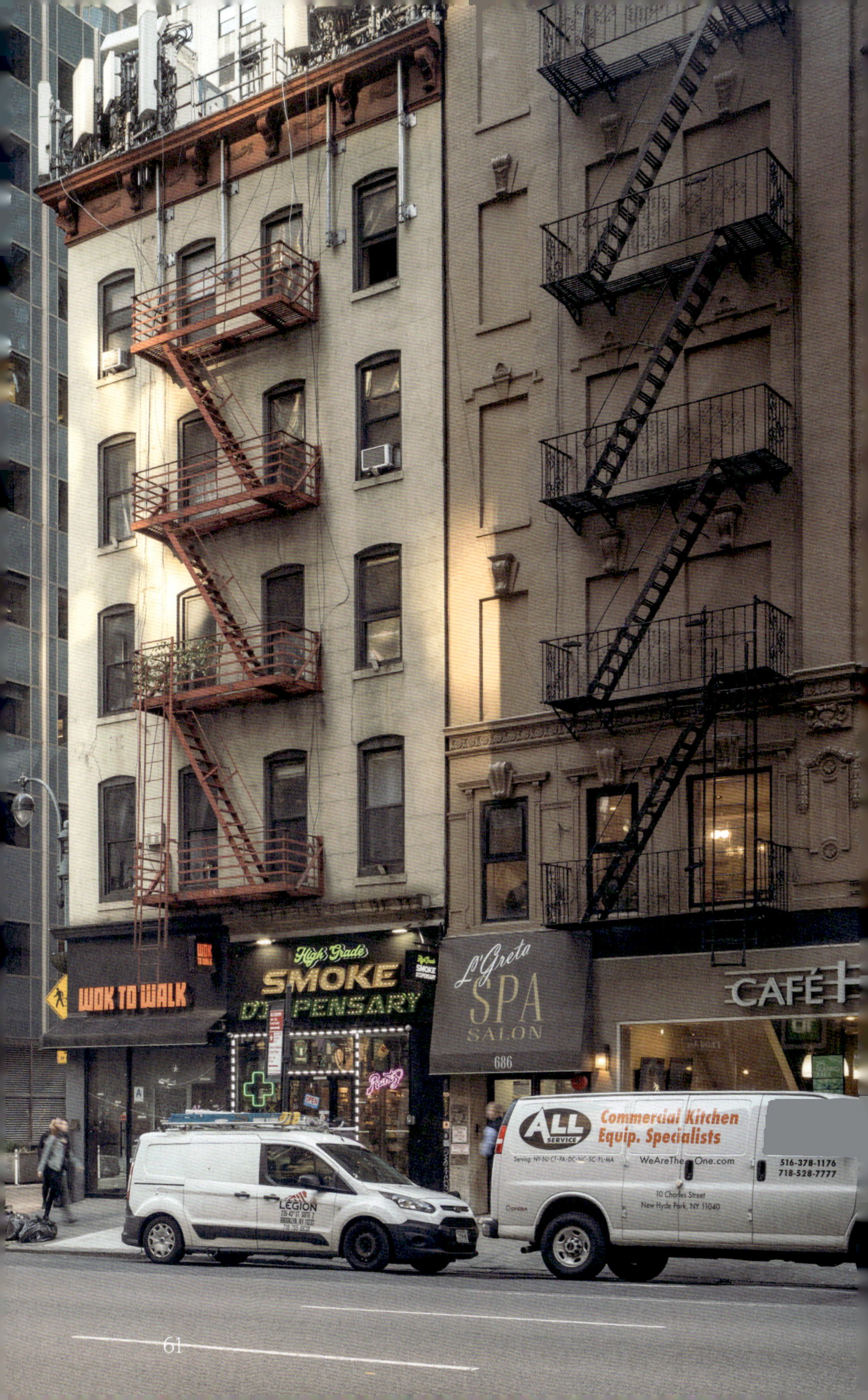
WOK TO WALK
High Grade
SMOKE
L'Greta
SPA
SALON
686
CAFÉ
ALL SERVICE
Commercial Kitchen
Equip. Specialists
516-378-1176
718-528-7777
10 Charles Street
New Hyde Park, NY 11040
LEGION

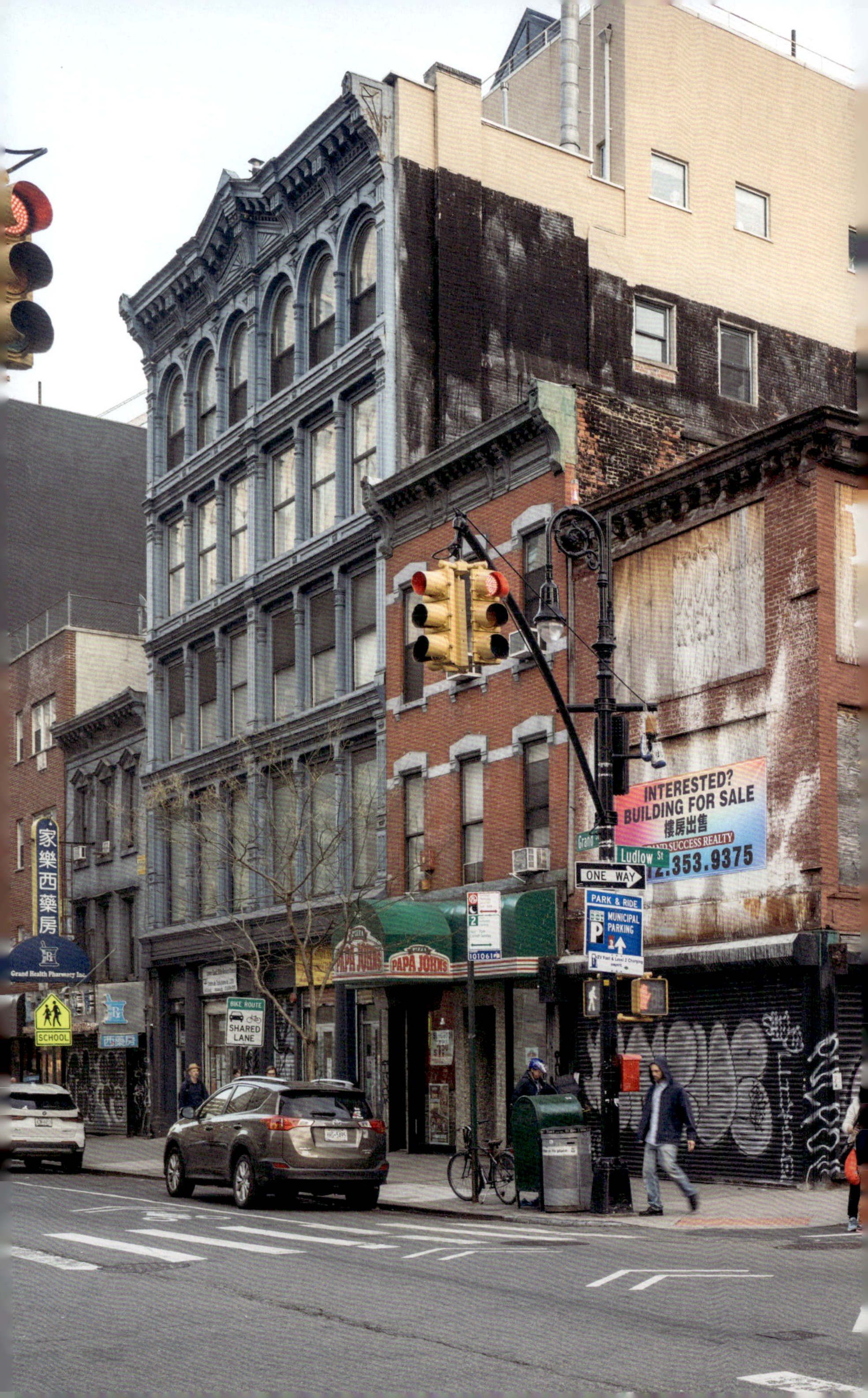
家樂西藥房
Grand Health Pharmacy Inc
SCHOOL
西藥房
BIKE ROUTE
SHARED LANE
PAPA JOHNS
PAPA JOHNS
INTERESTED?
BUILDING FOR SALE
樓房出售
.353.9375
Ludlow St
ONE WAY
PARK & RIDE
MUNICIPAL
PARKING

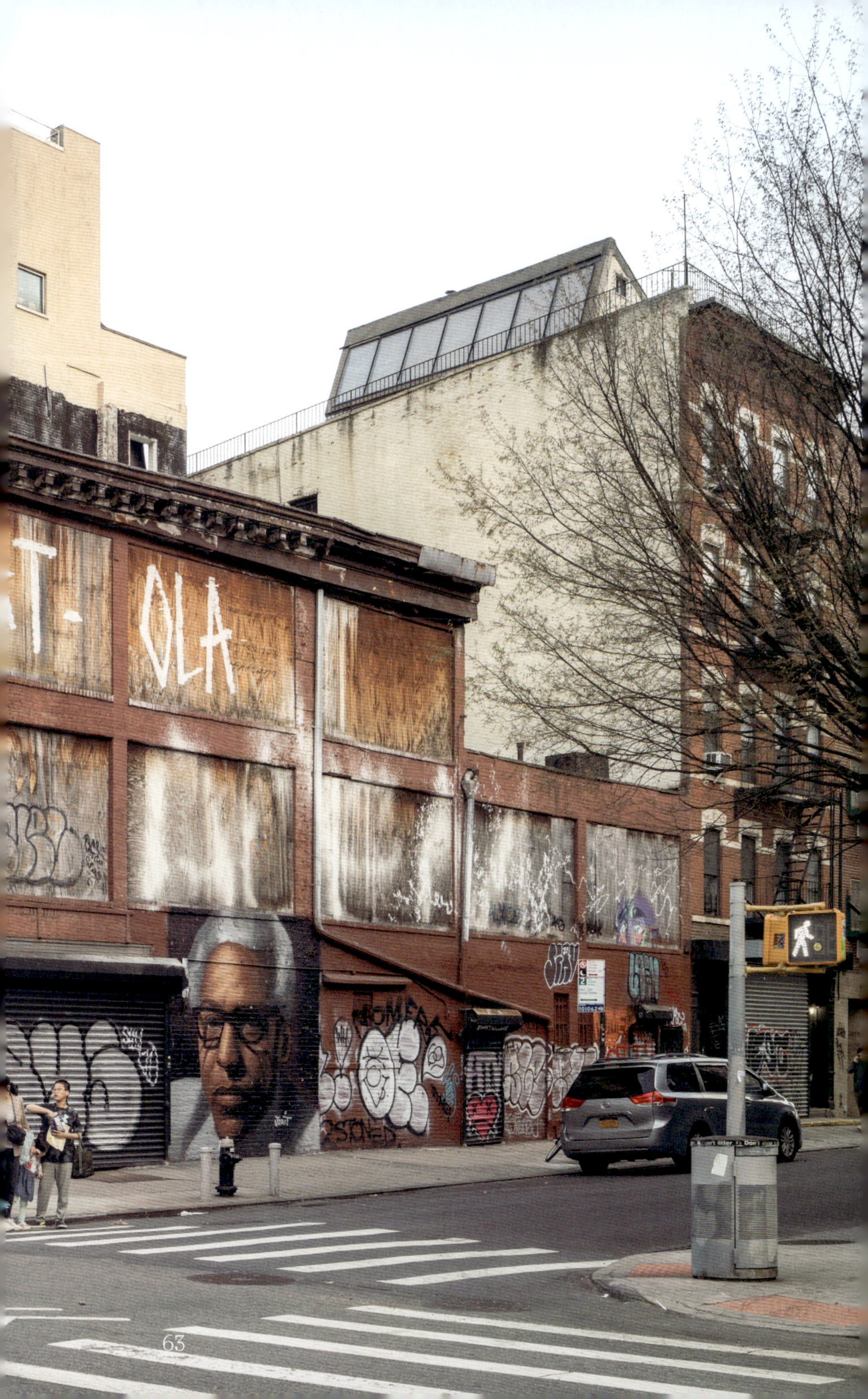
OLA

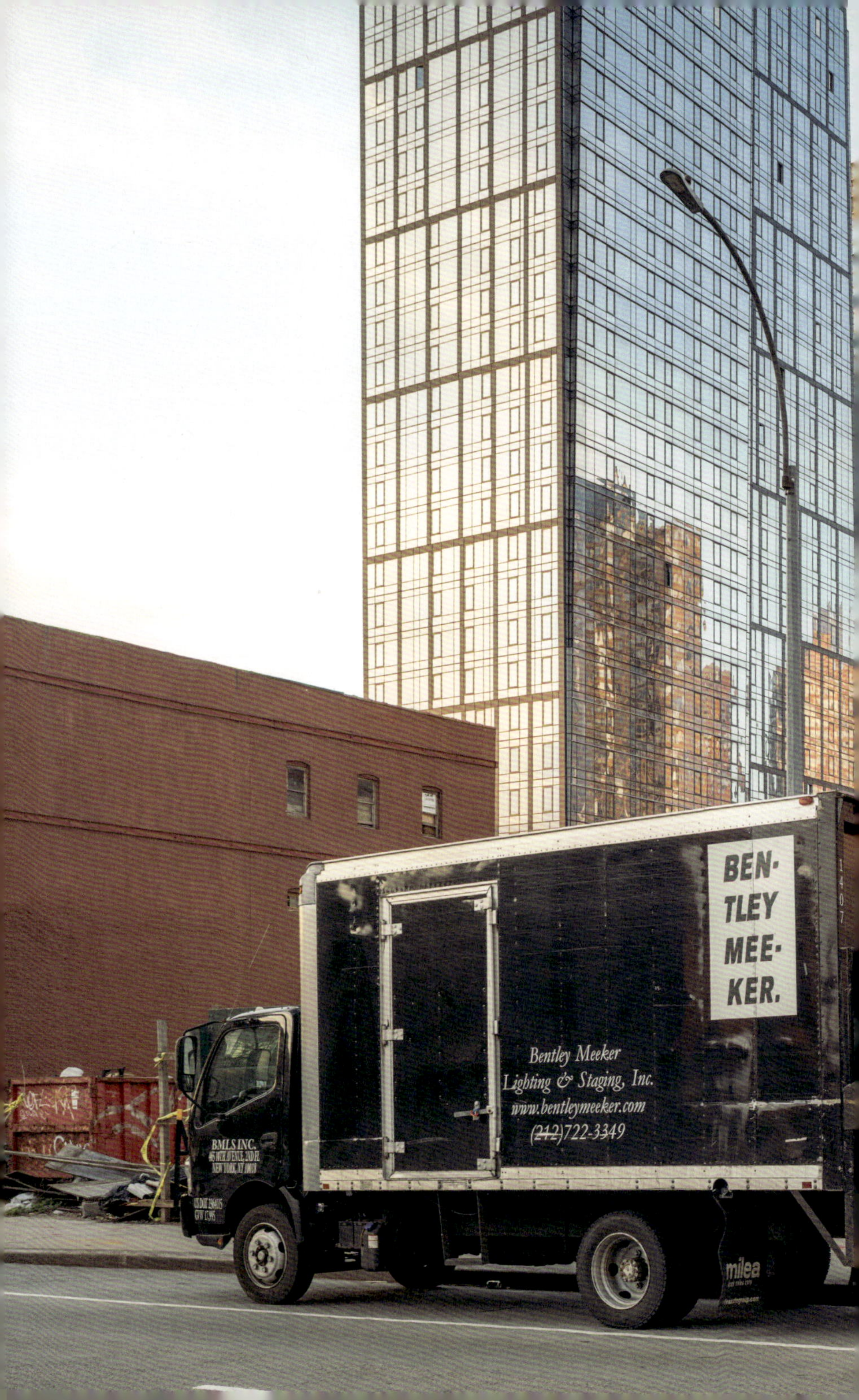
BEN-
TLEY
MEE-
KER.
Bentley Meeker
Lighting & Staging, Inc.
www.bentleymeeker.com
(212)722-3349
BMLS INC.
milea

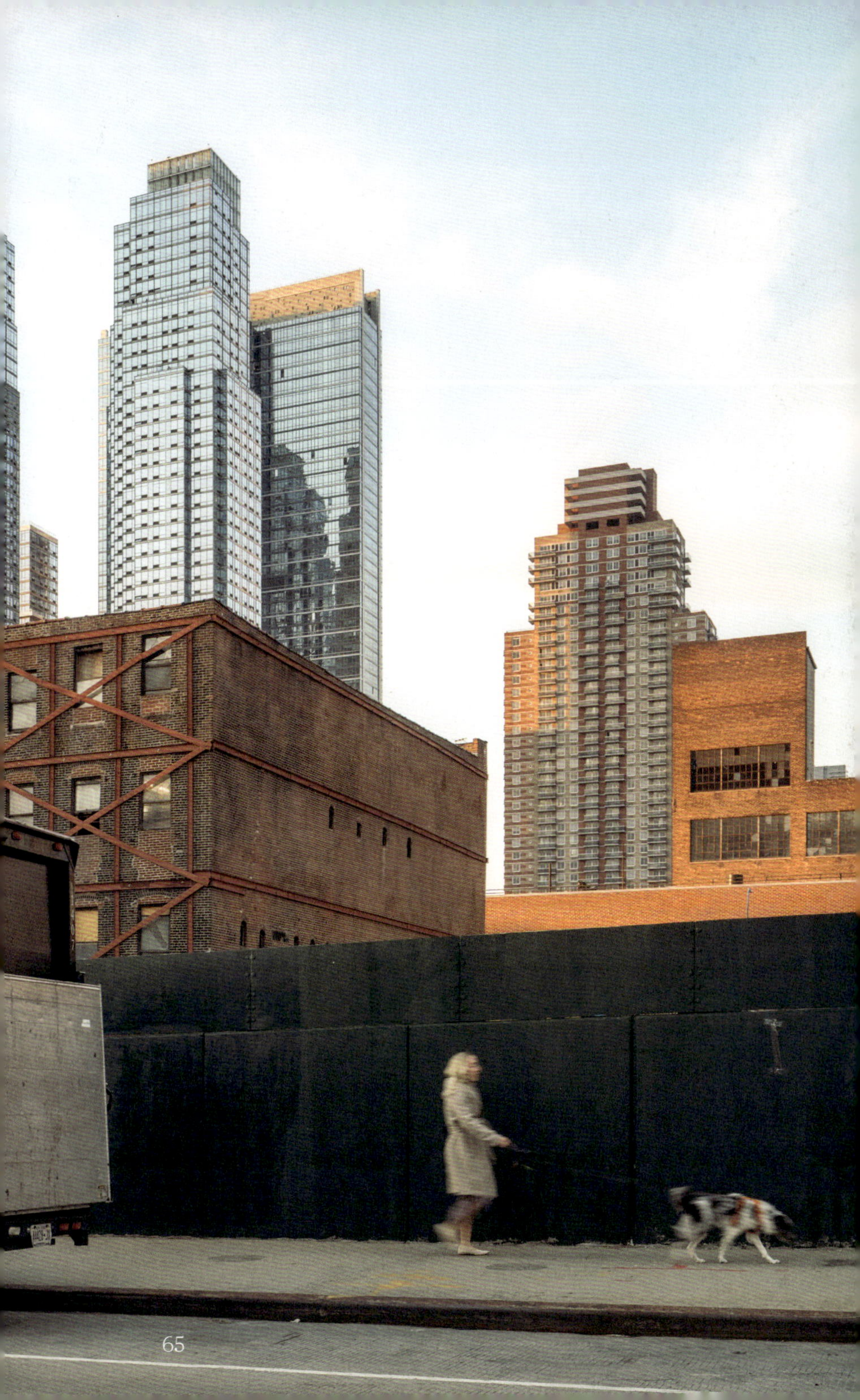

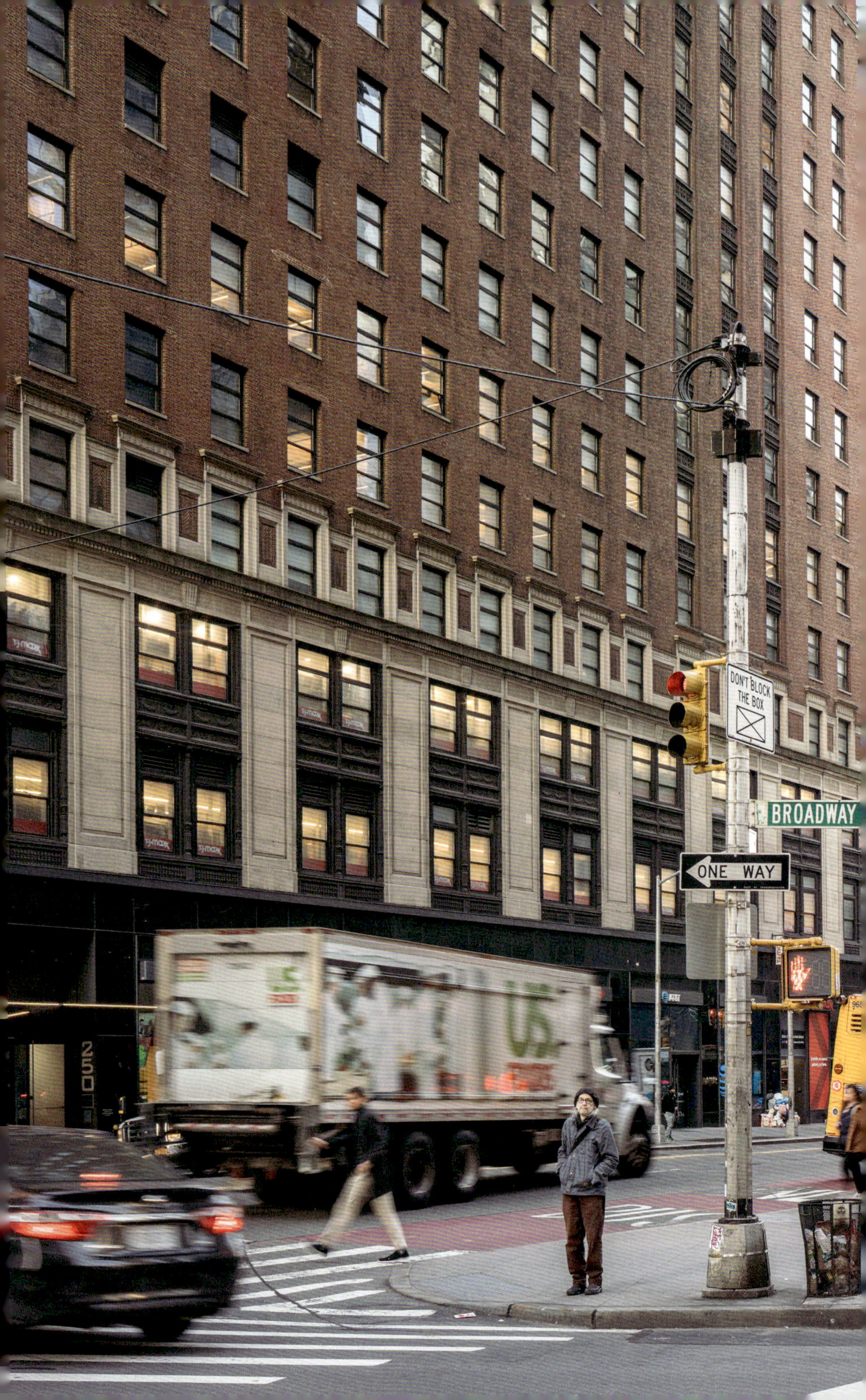

DON'T BLOCK THE BOX
BROADWAY
ONE WAY
250

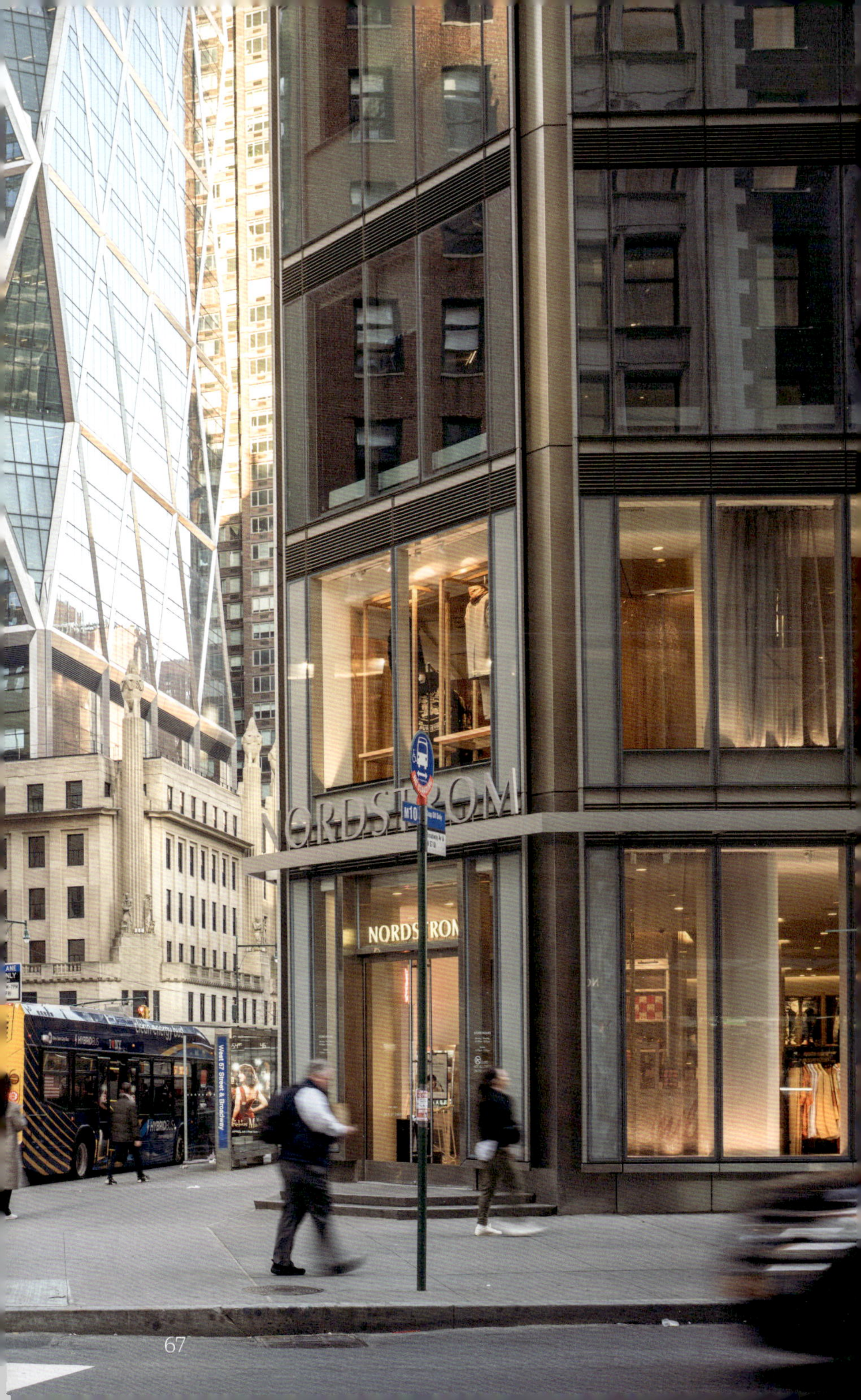
NORDSTROM
NORDSTROM
M10
West 57 Street & Broadway

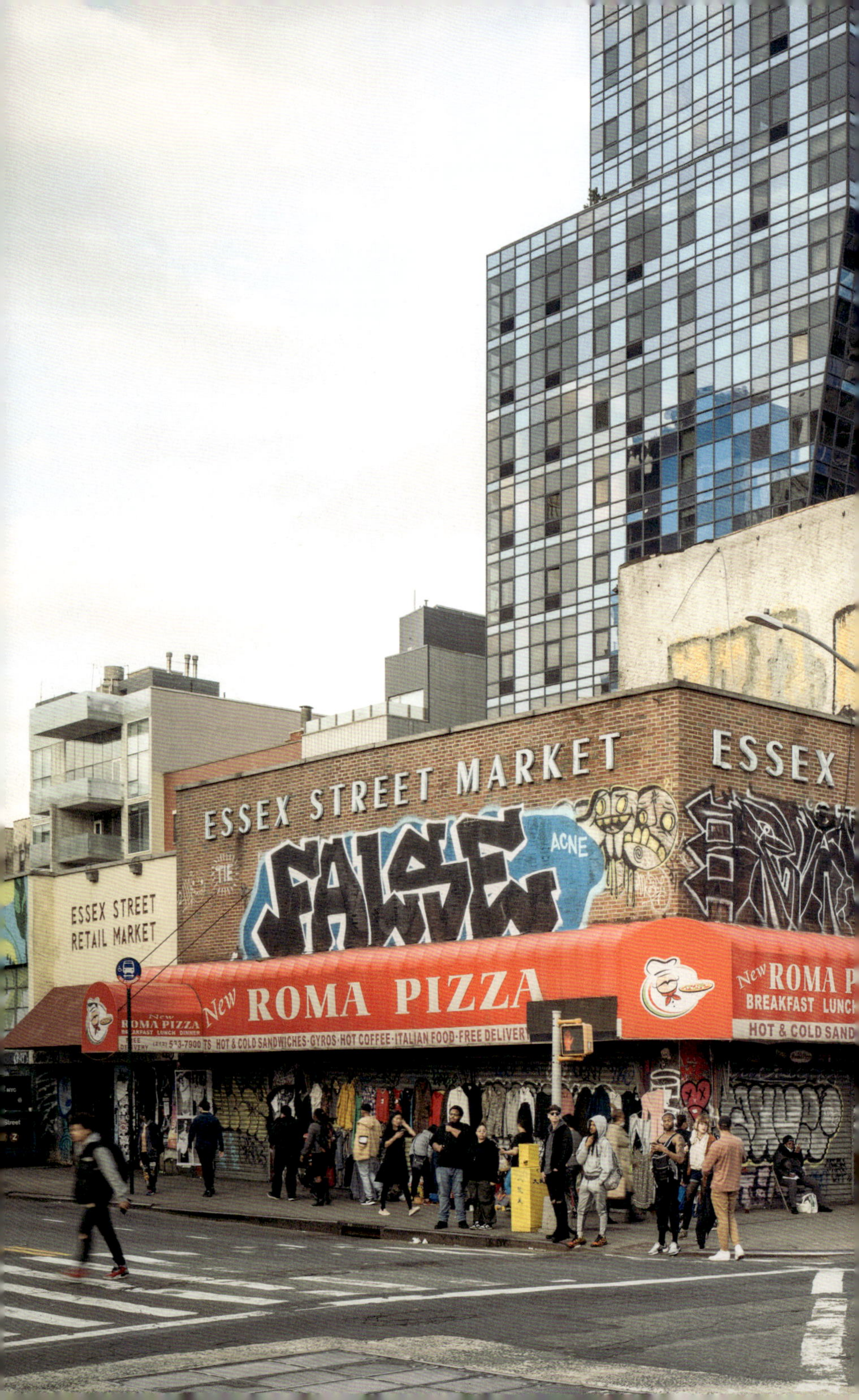
ESSEX STREET MARKET
ESSEX
ESSEX STREET
RETAIL MARKET
New ROMA PIZZA
HOT & COLD SANDWICHES · GYROS · HOT COFFEE · ITALIAN FOOD · FREE DELIVERY

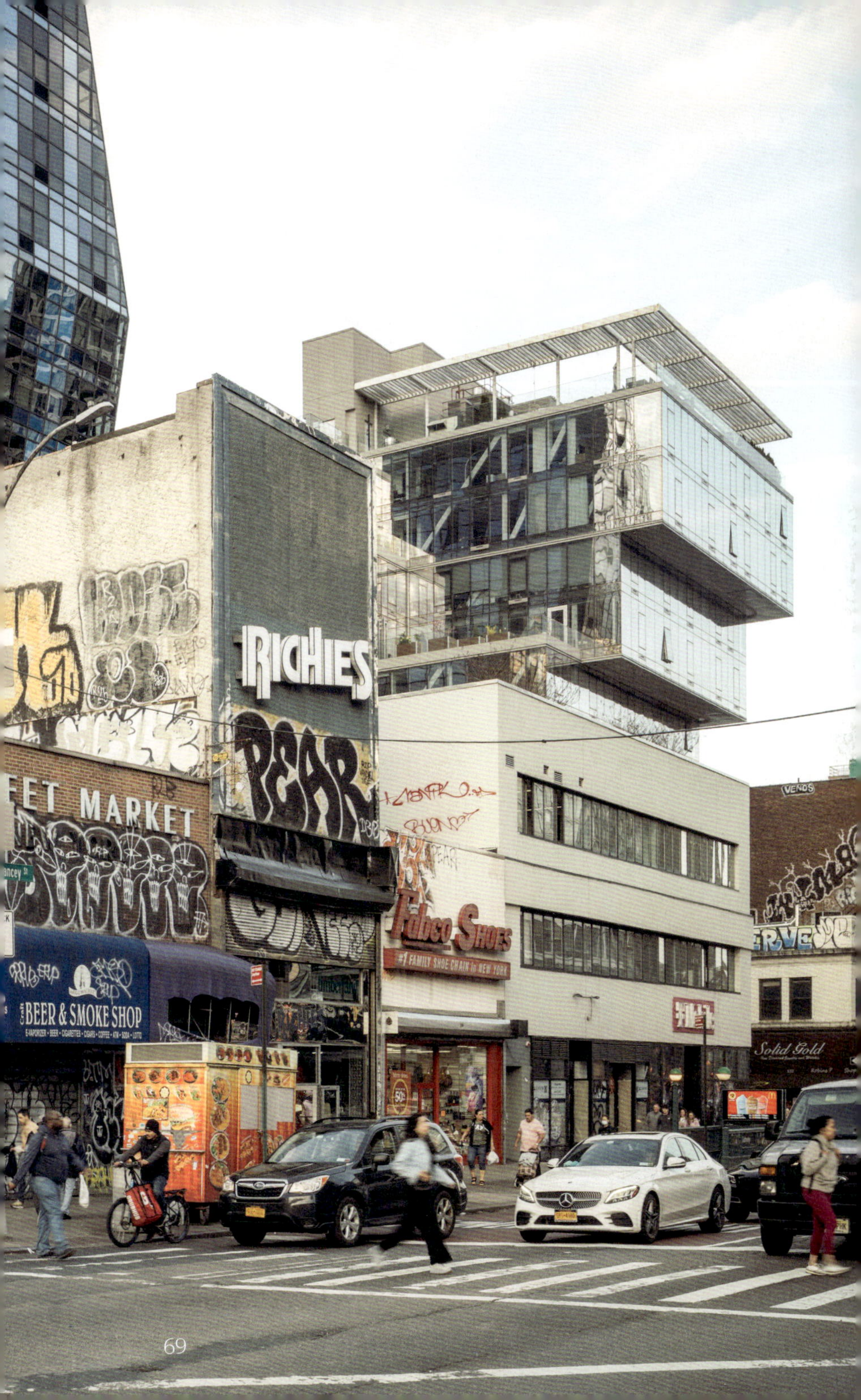
RICHIES
PEAR
FET MARKET
BEER & SMOKE SHOP
Fabco SHOES
#1 FAMILY SHOE CHAIN in NEW YORK
Solid Gold

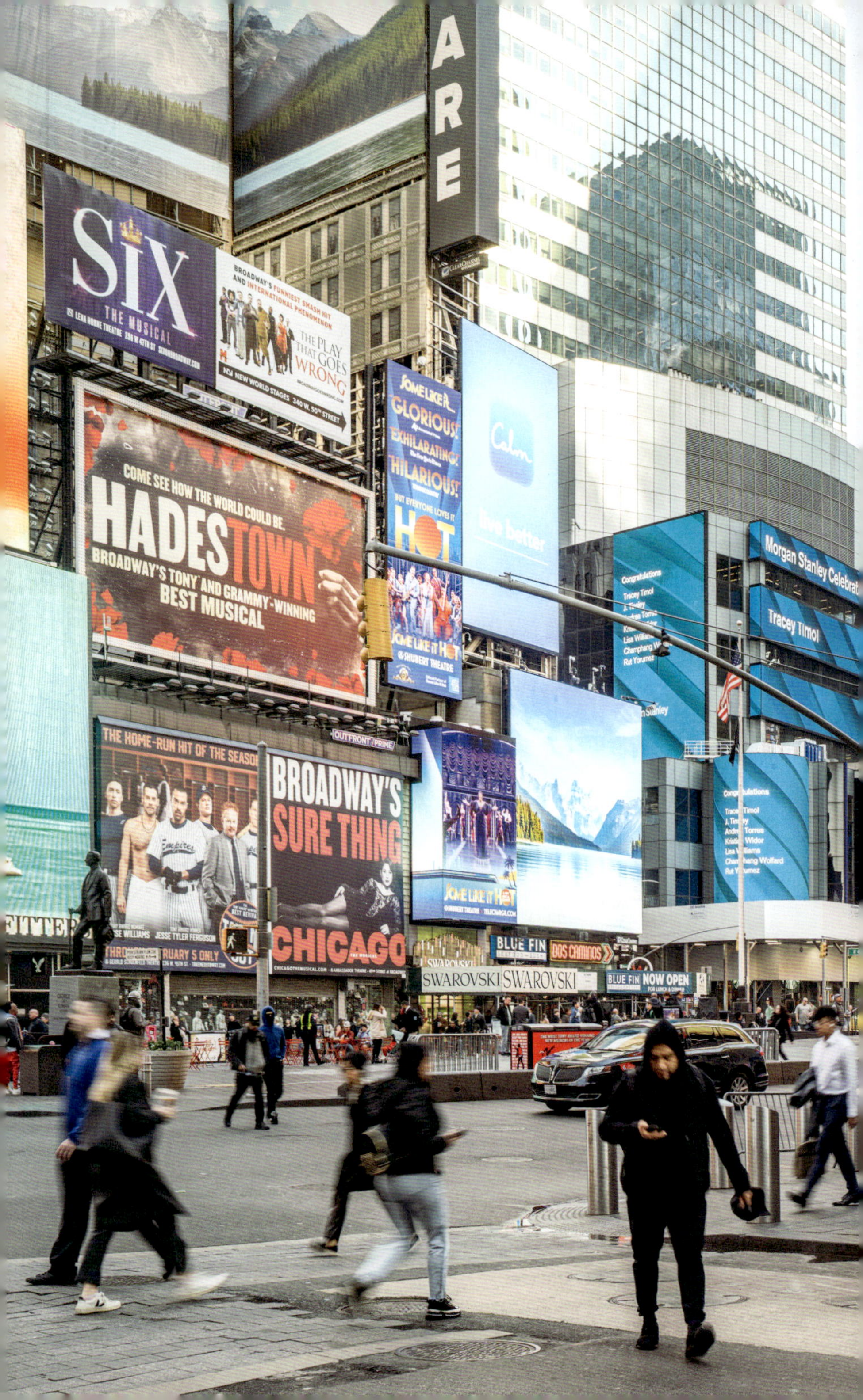
SIX
THE MUSICAL
BROADWAY'S FUNNIEST SMASH HIT AND INTERNATIONAL PHENOMENON
THE PLAY THAT GOES WRONG
NEW WORLD STAGES 340 W. 50TH STREET
COME SEE HOW THE WORLD COULD BE.
HADESTOWN
BROADWAY'S TONY AND GRAMMY-WINNING
BEST MUSICAL
SOME LIKE IT GLORIOUS!
EXHILARATING!
HILARIOUS!
BUT EVERYONE LOVES IT HOT
SOME LIKE IT HOT
SHUBERT THEATRE
Calm
live better
Morgan Stanley Celebrat
Tracey Timol
Congratulations
THE HOME-RUN HIT OF THE SEASON
BROADWAY'S SURE THING
CHICAGO
OUTFRONT PRIME
SWAROVSKI SWAROVSKI
BLUE FIN
NOW OPEN
DOS CAMINOS

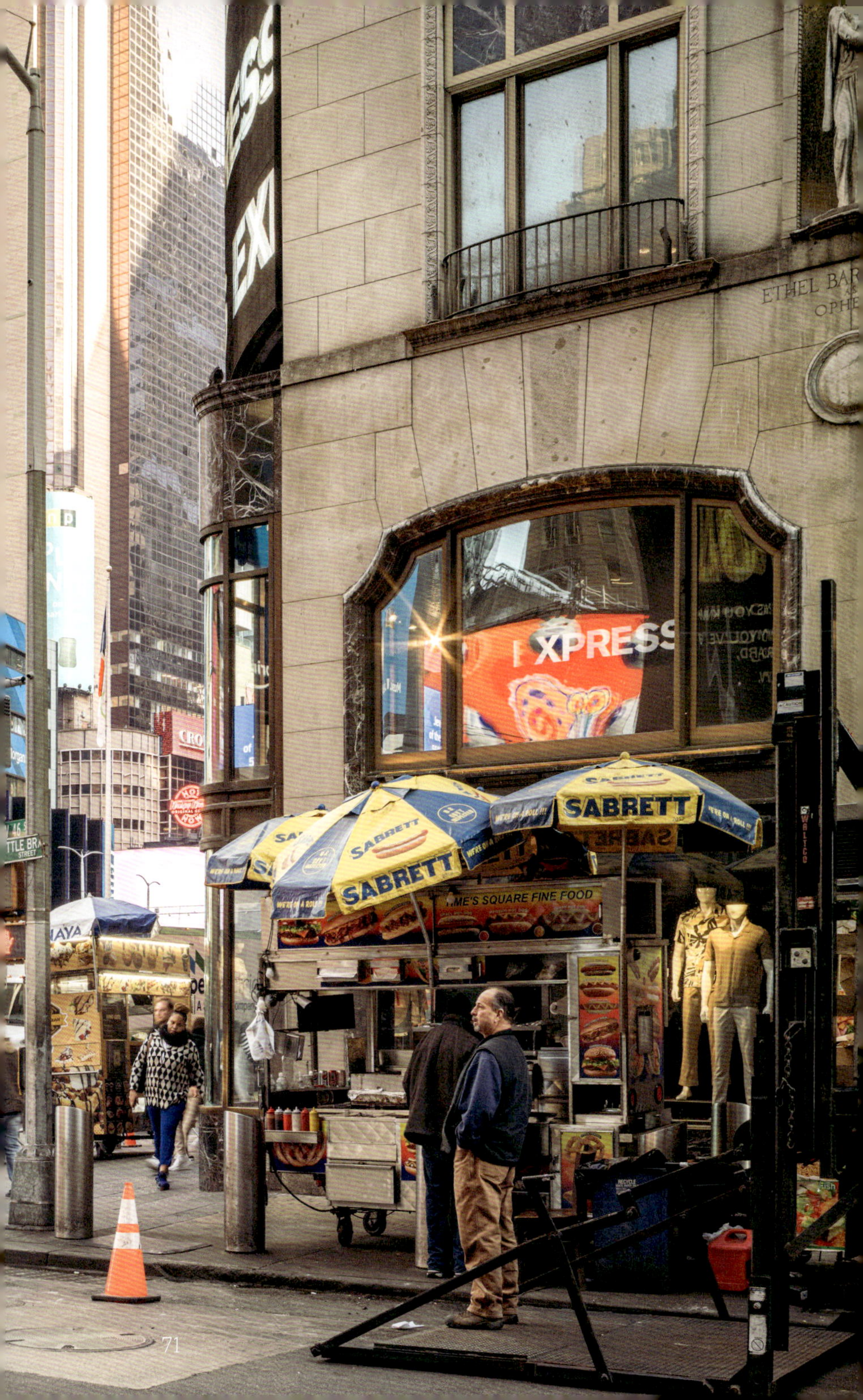
XPRESS
SABRETT
SABRETT
SABRETT
IME'S SQUARE FINE FOOD

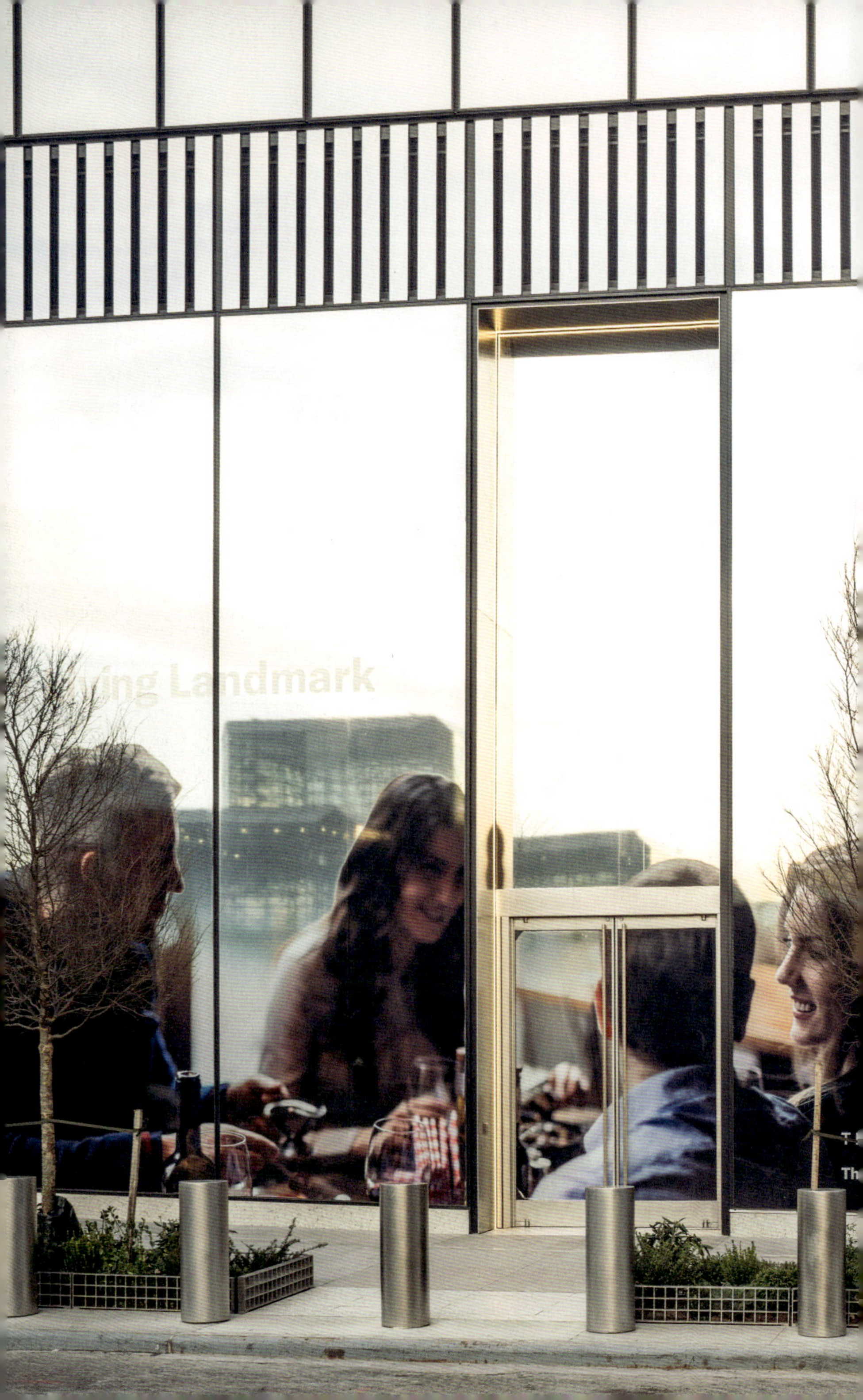
Landmark

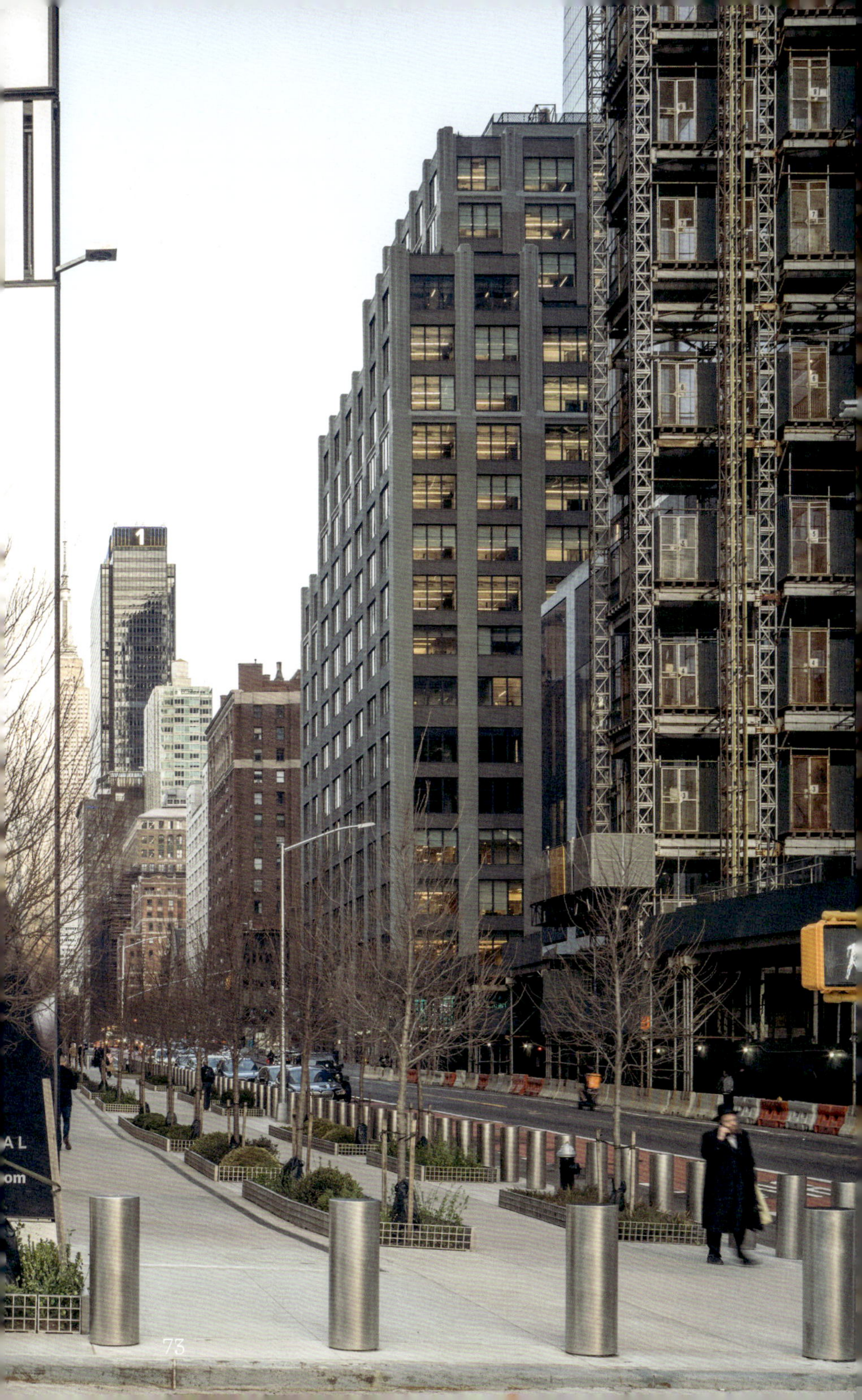

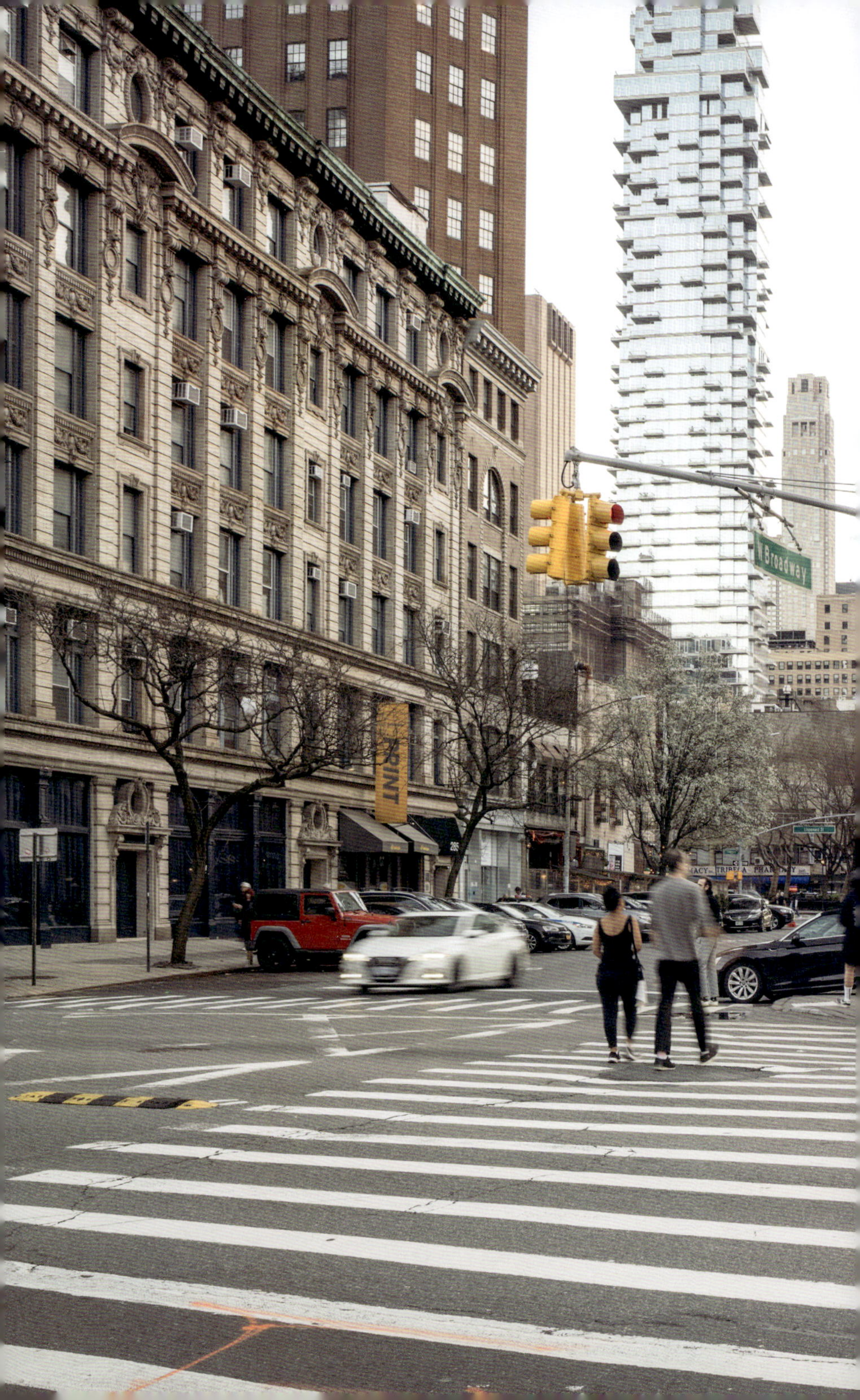
W Broadway

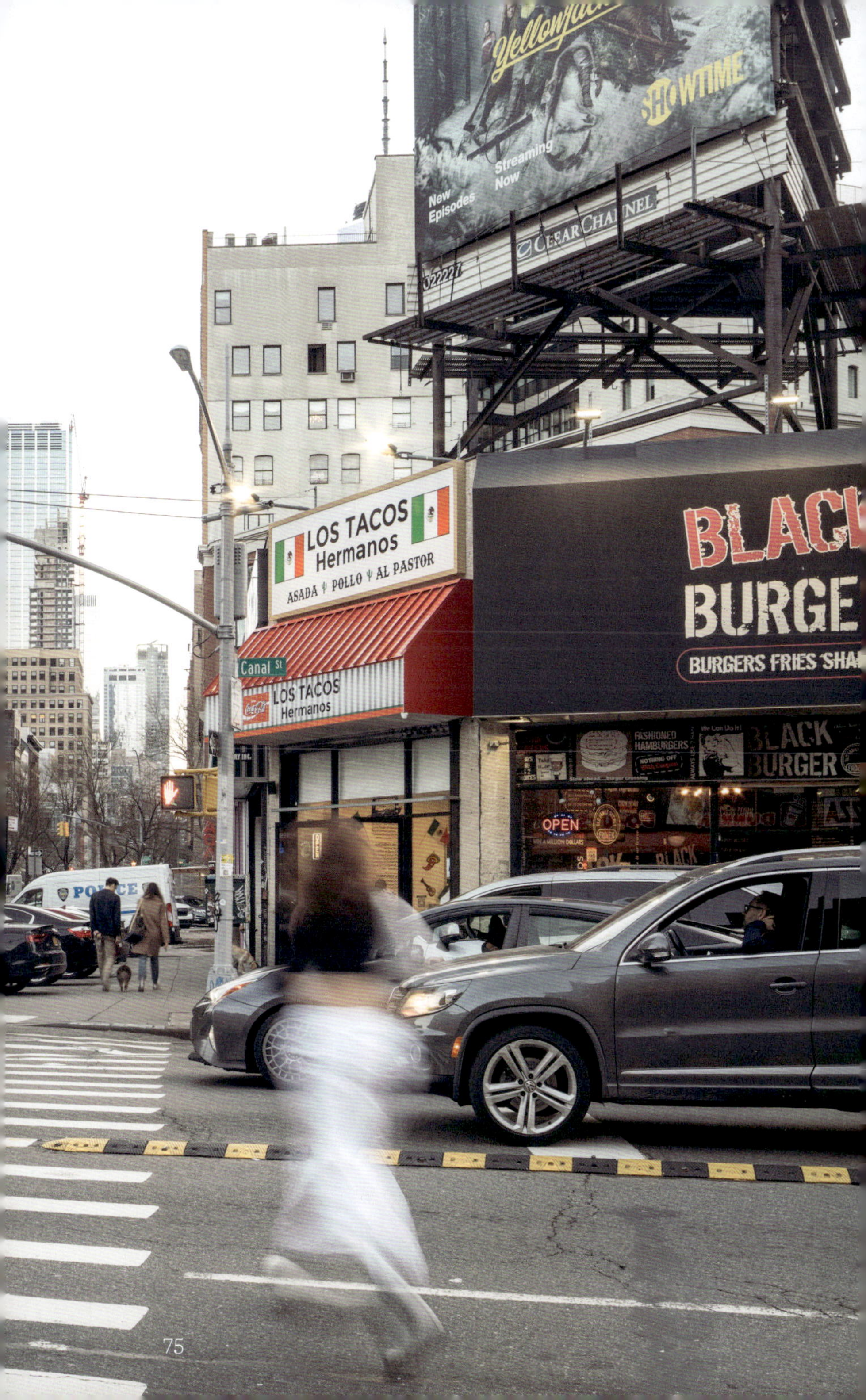
Yellowjackets
SHOWTIME
New Episodes
Streaming Now
CLEAR CHANNEL
LOS TACOS
Hermanos
ASADA POLLO AL PASTOR
Canal St
LOS TACOS
Hermanos
BLACK
BURGER
BURGERS FRIES SHA
BLACK
BURGER
OPEN
POLICE

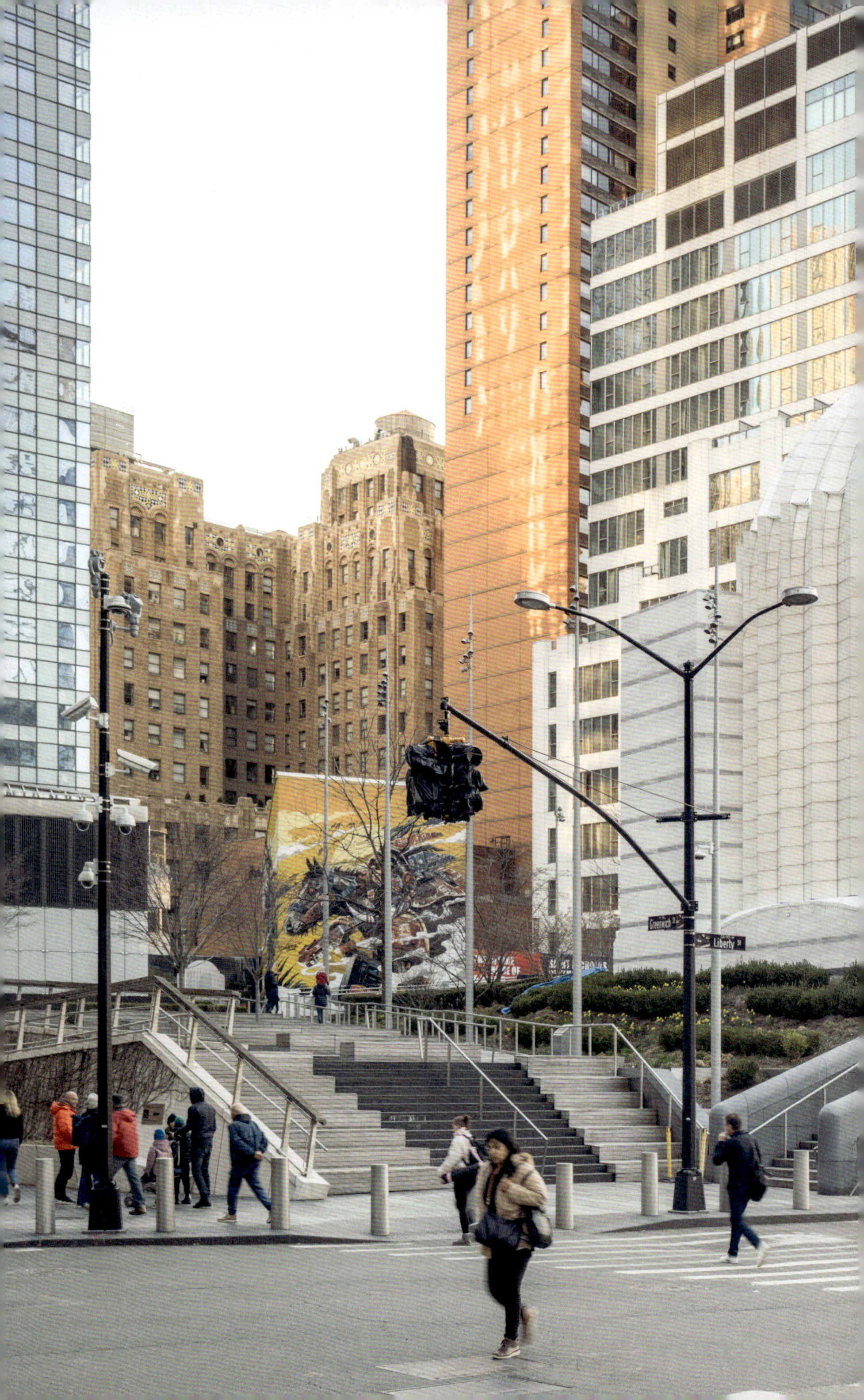
Greenwich St
Liberty St

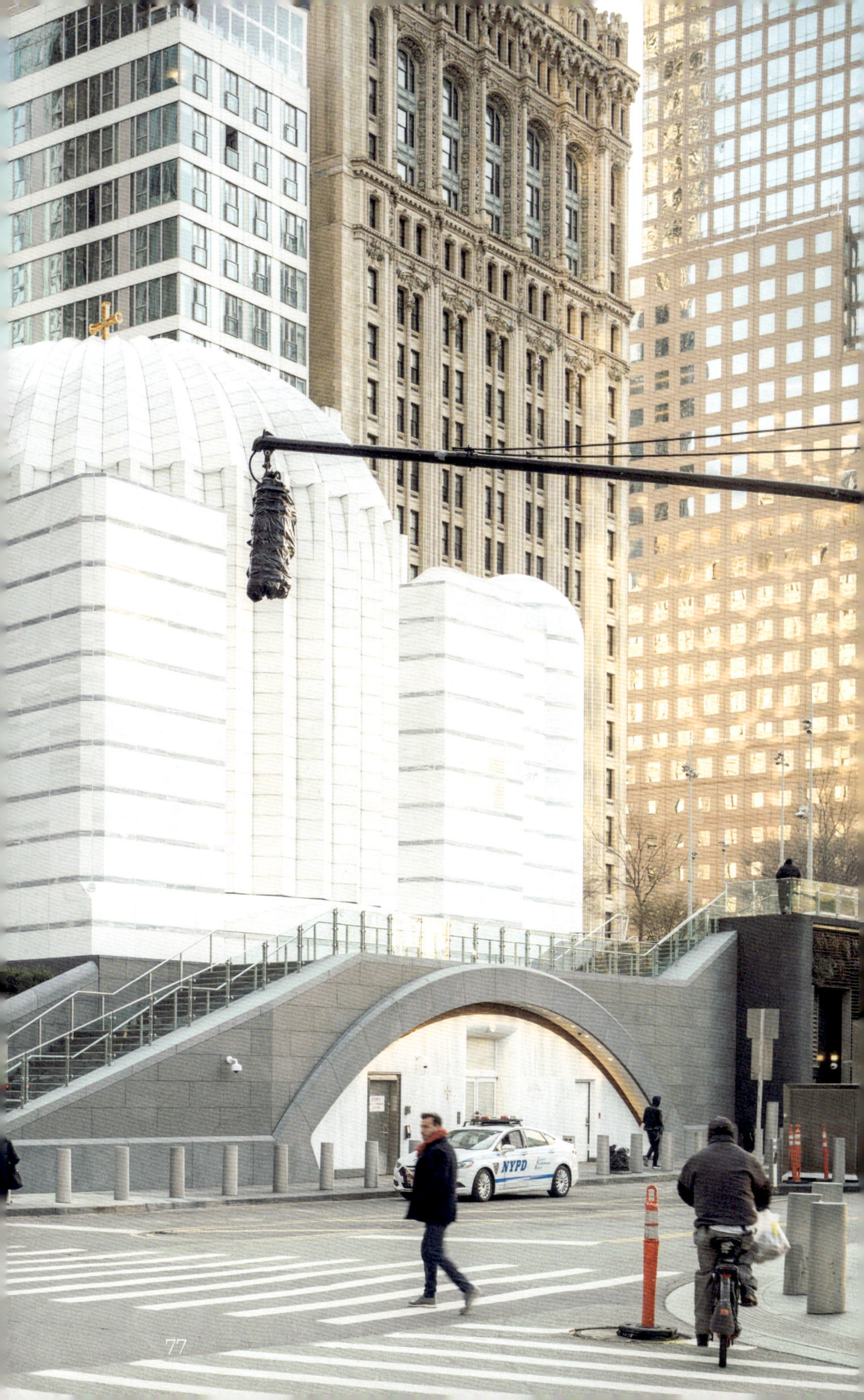
NYPD

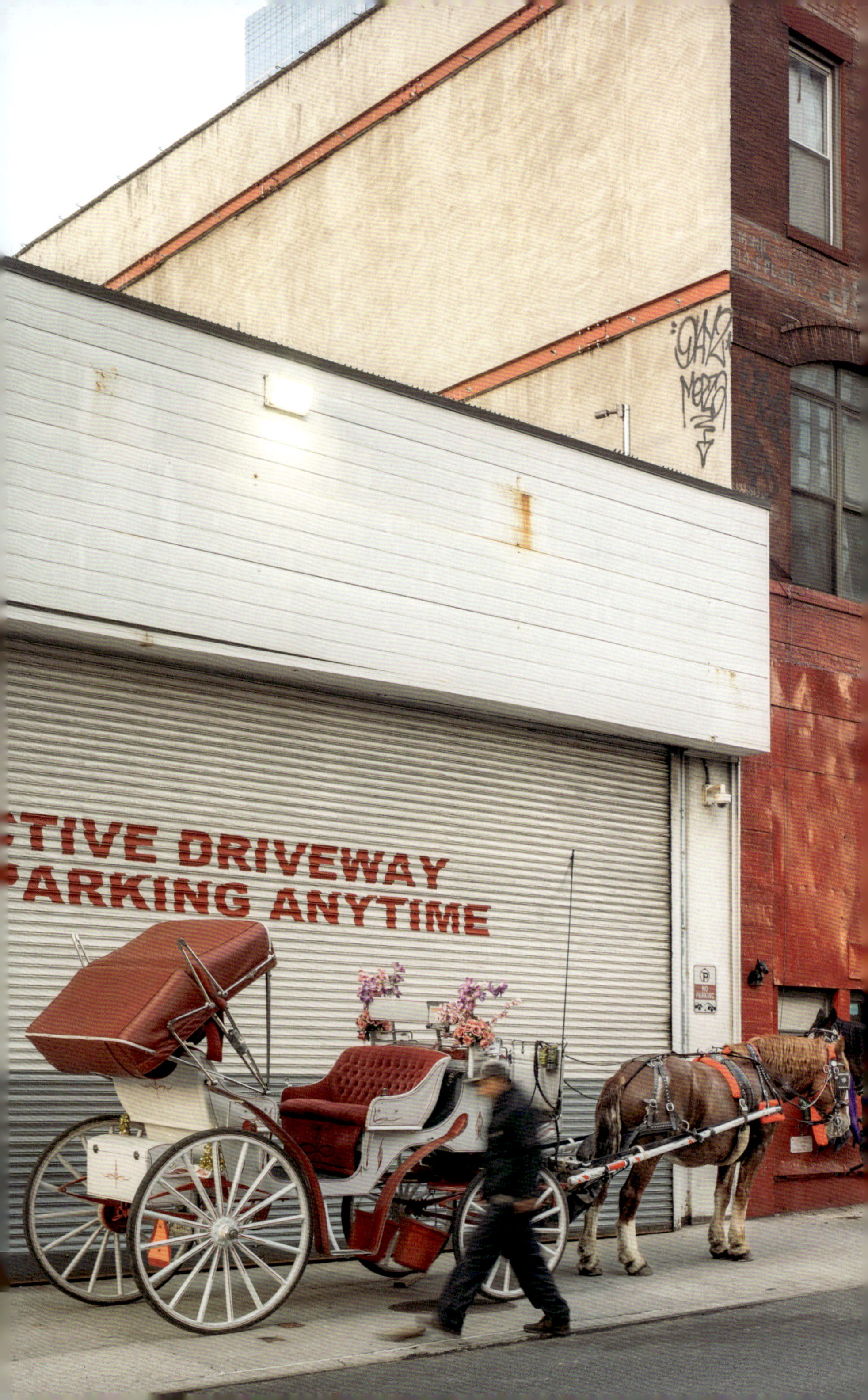
CTIVE DRIVEWAY
ARKING ANYTIME

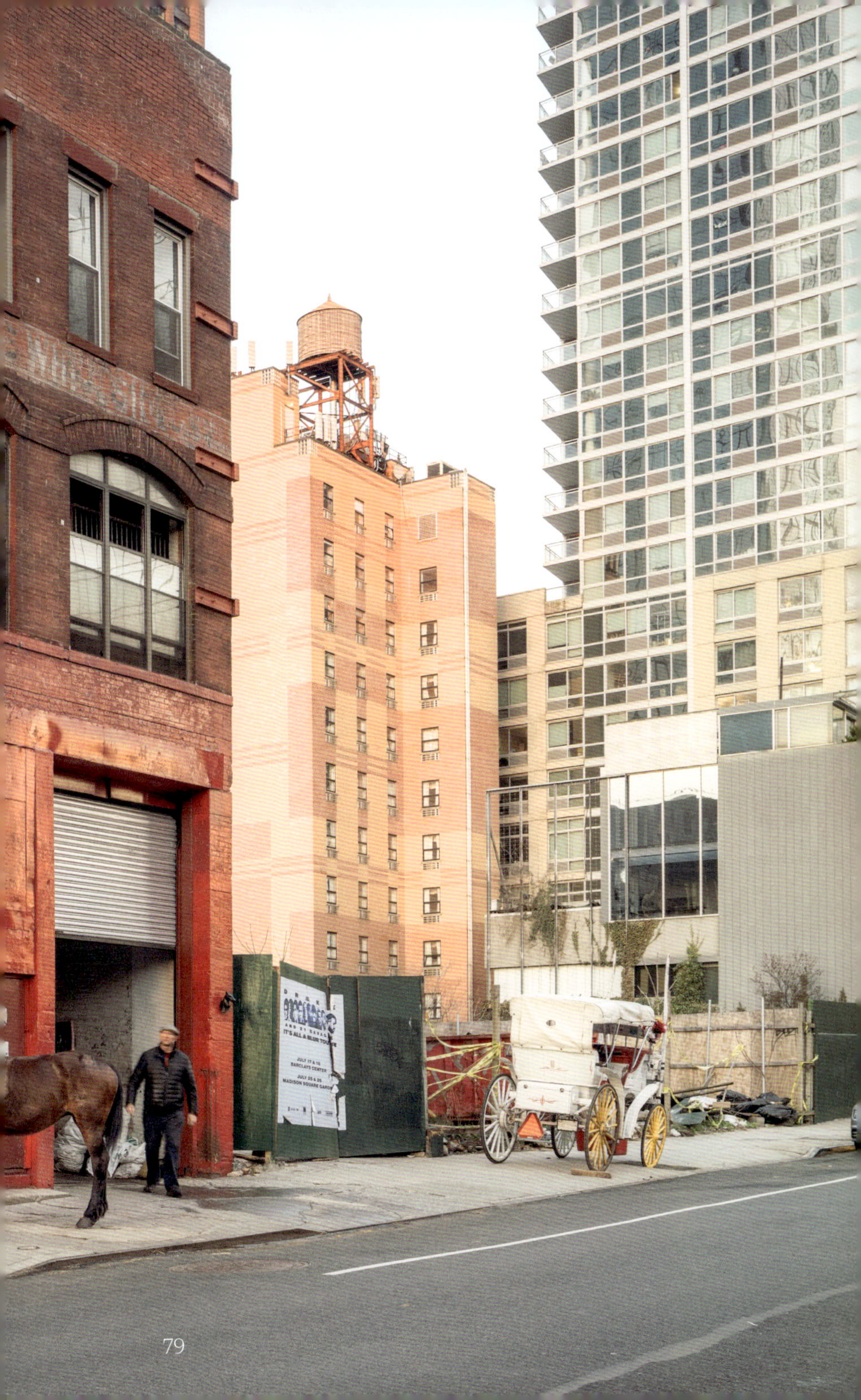
BARCLAYS CENTER

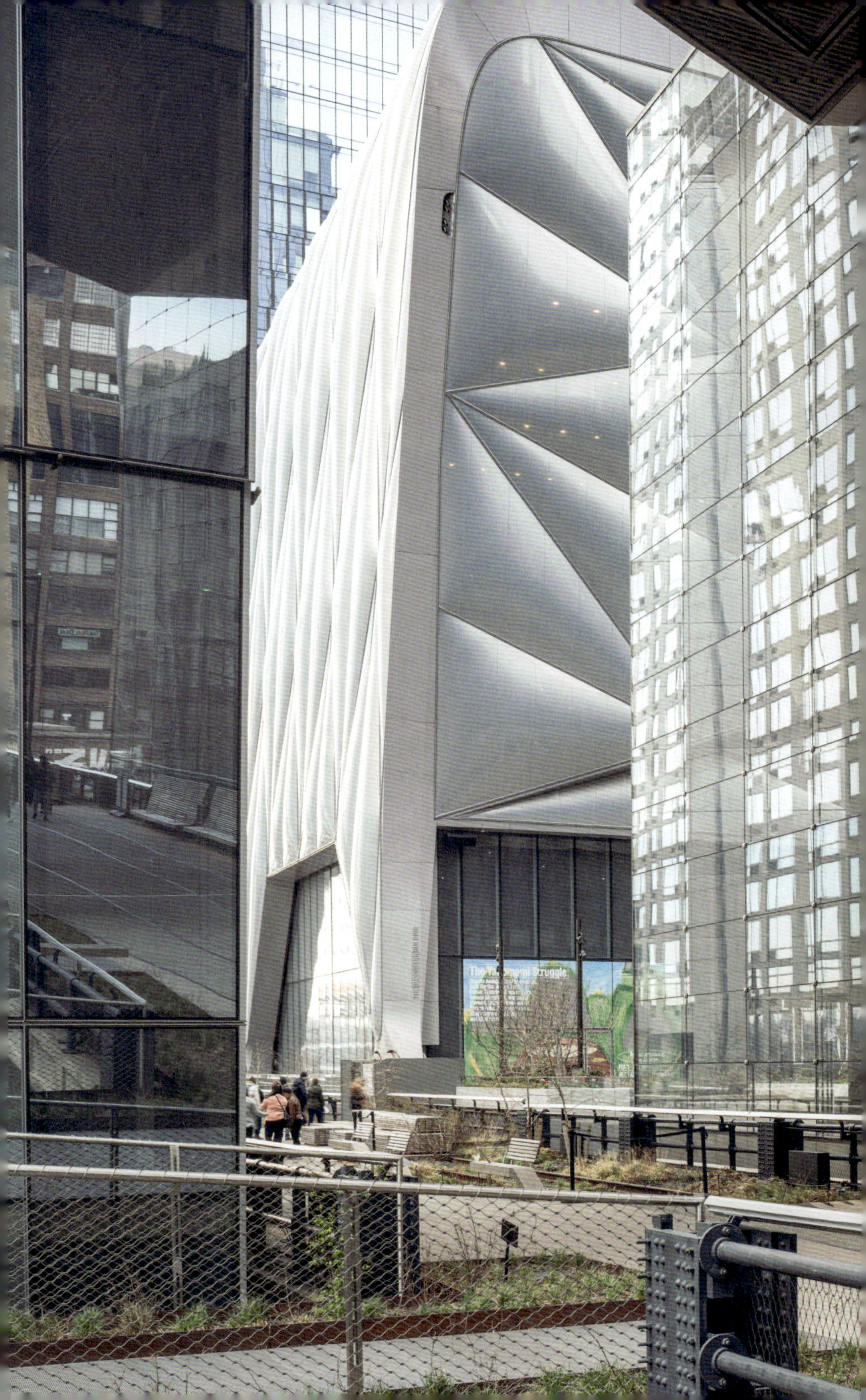

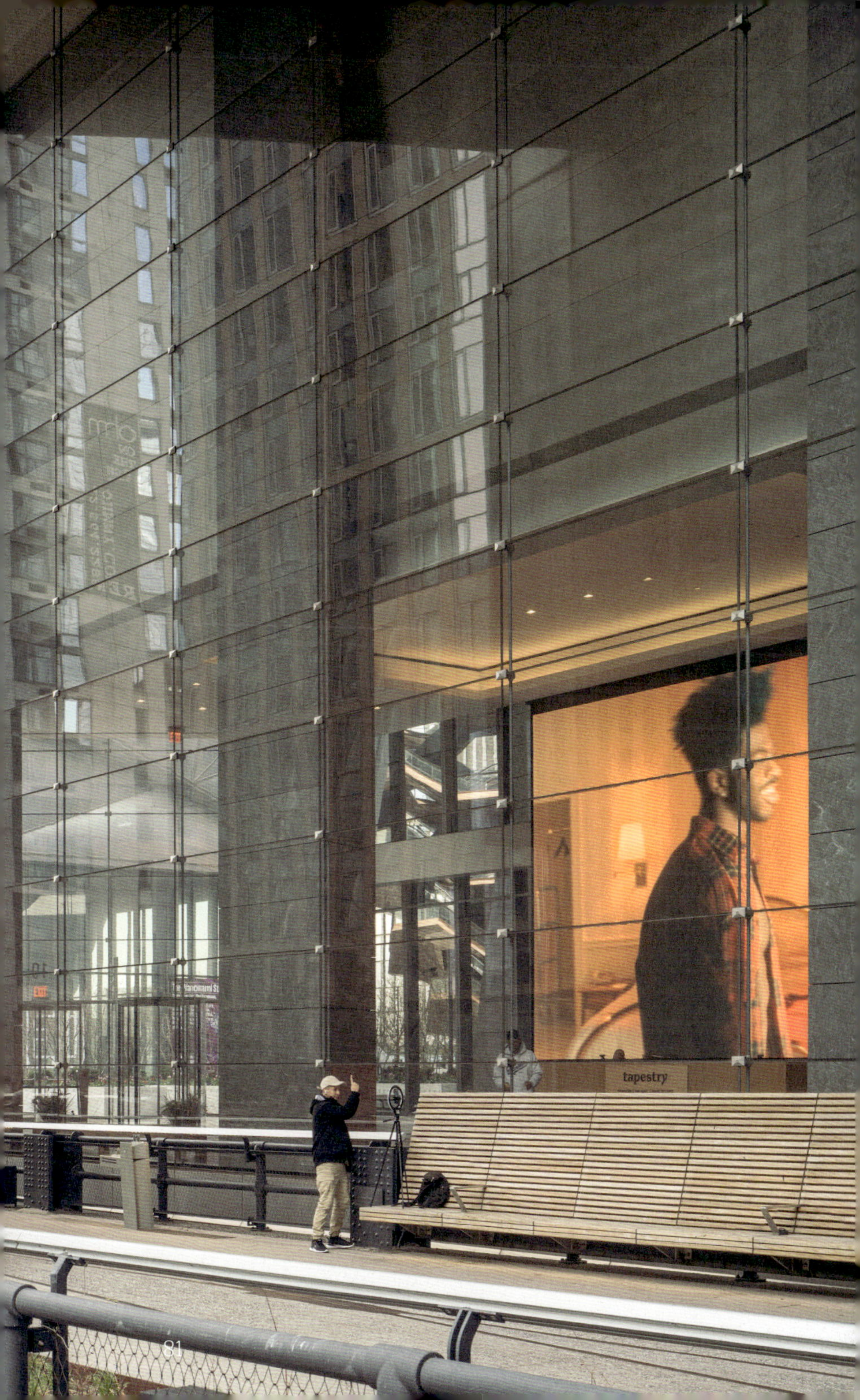
tapestry

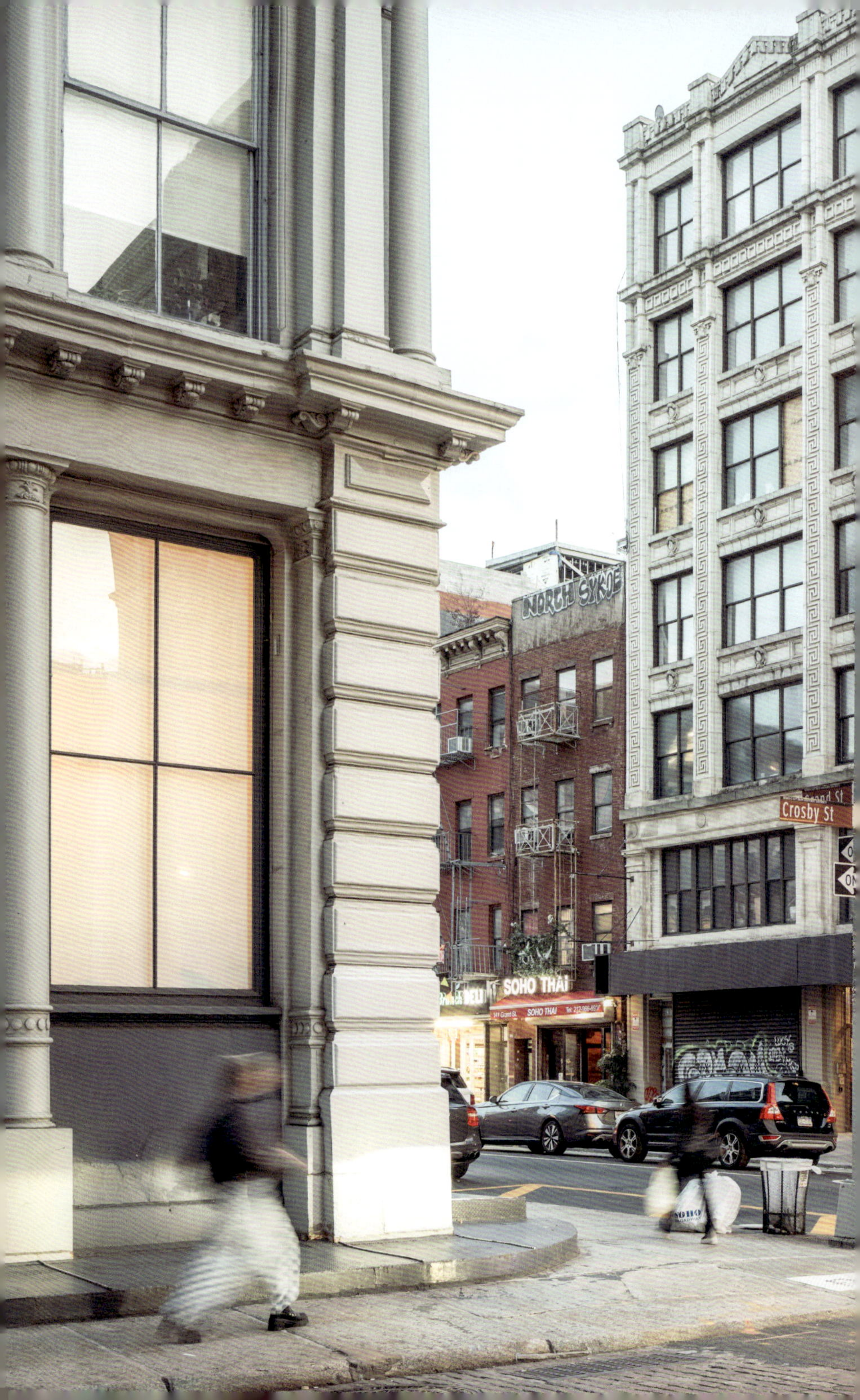
NORTH SYKOE
SOHO THAI
SOHO THAI
DELI
Crosby St

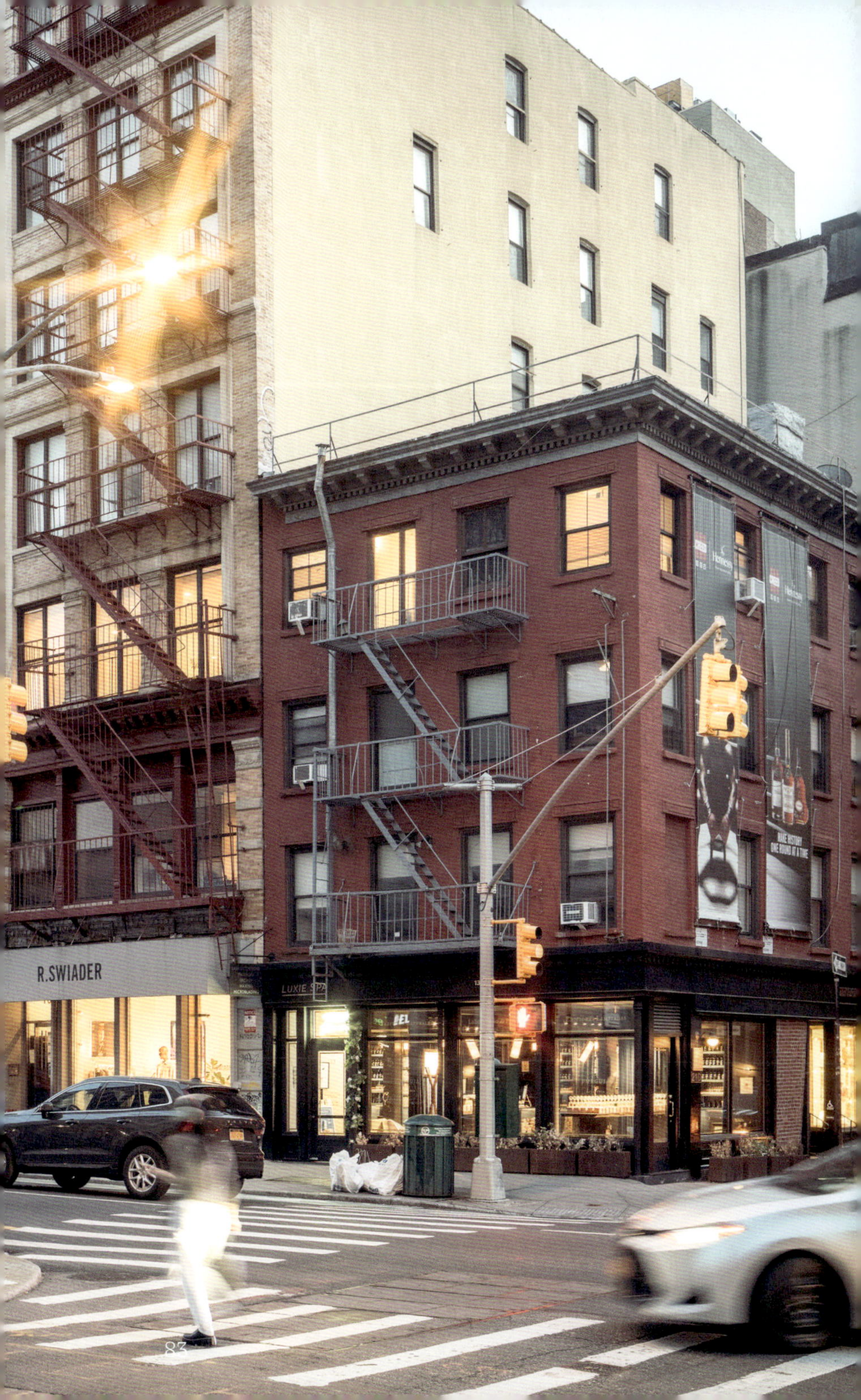
R.SWIADER
LUXIE SPA
MAKE HISTORY
ONE ROUND AT A TIME

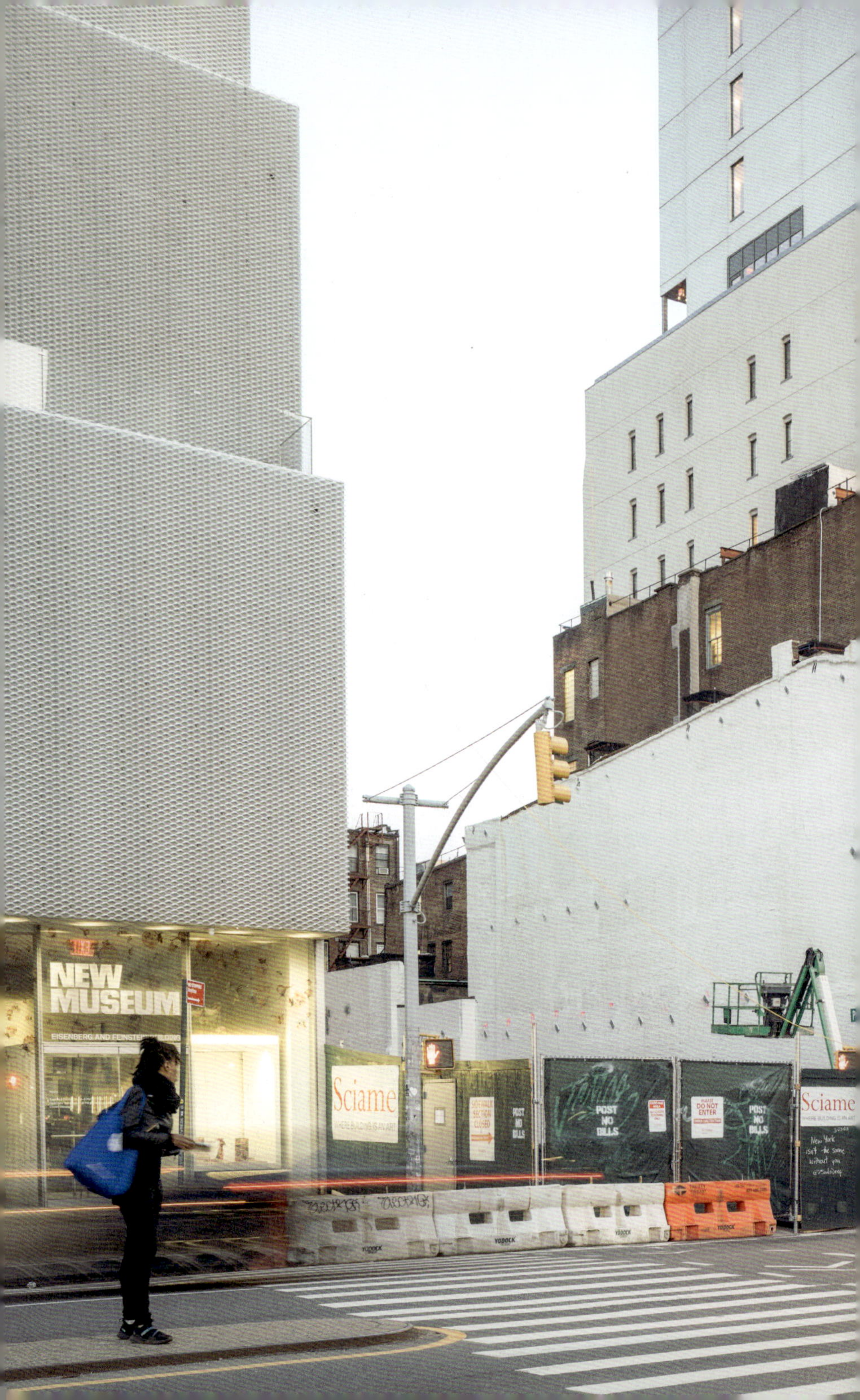
NEW MUSEUM
Sciame
POST NO BILLS
DO NOT ENTER
POST NO BILLS
Sciame
New York isn't the same without you

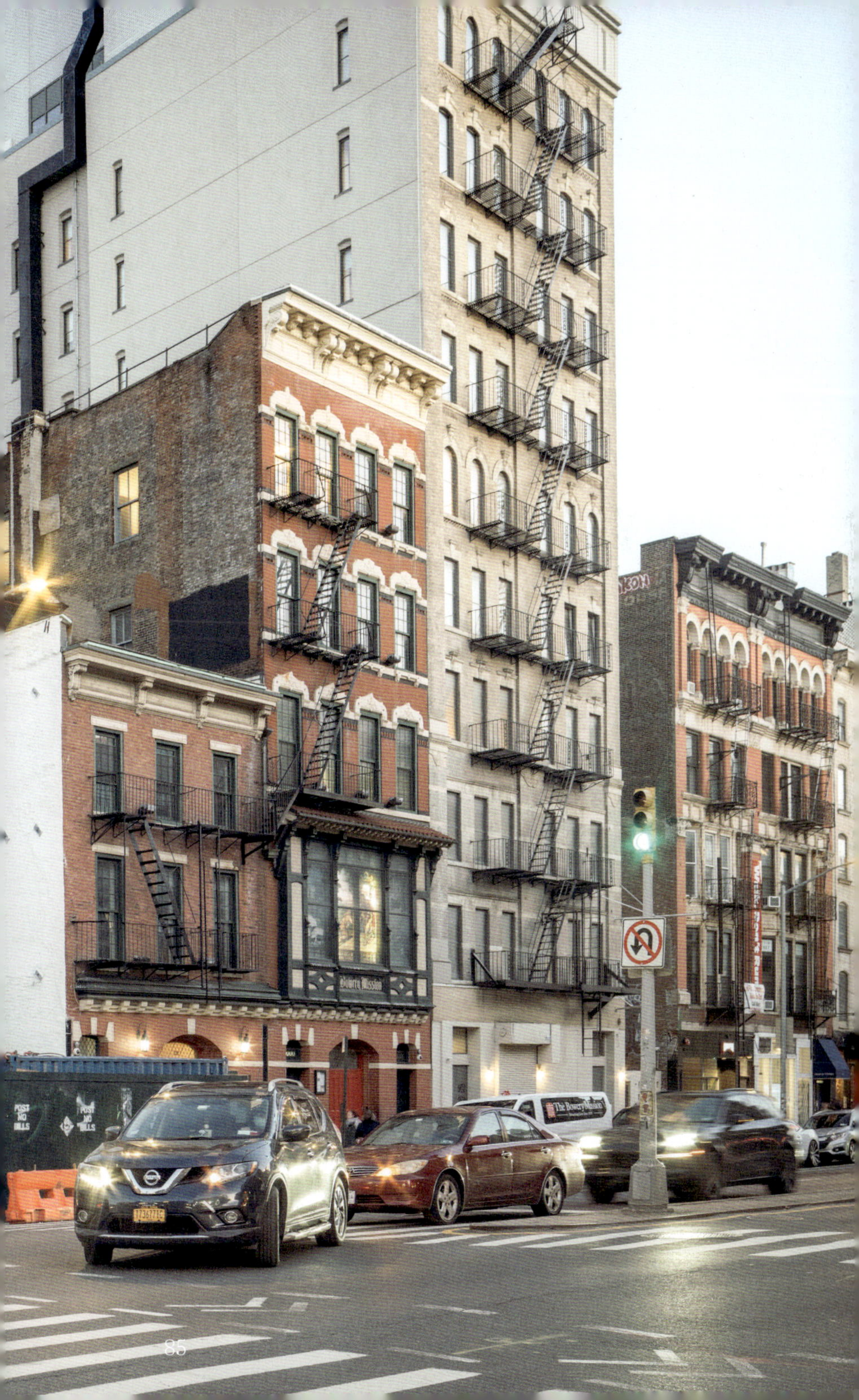
POST NO BILLS
POST NO BILLS
Bowery Mission
The Bowery Mission

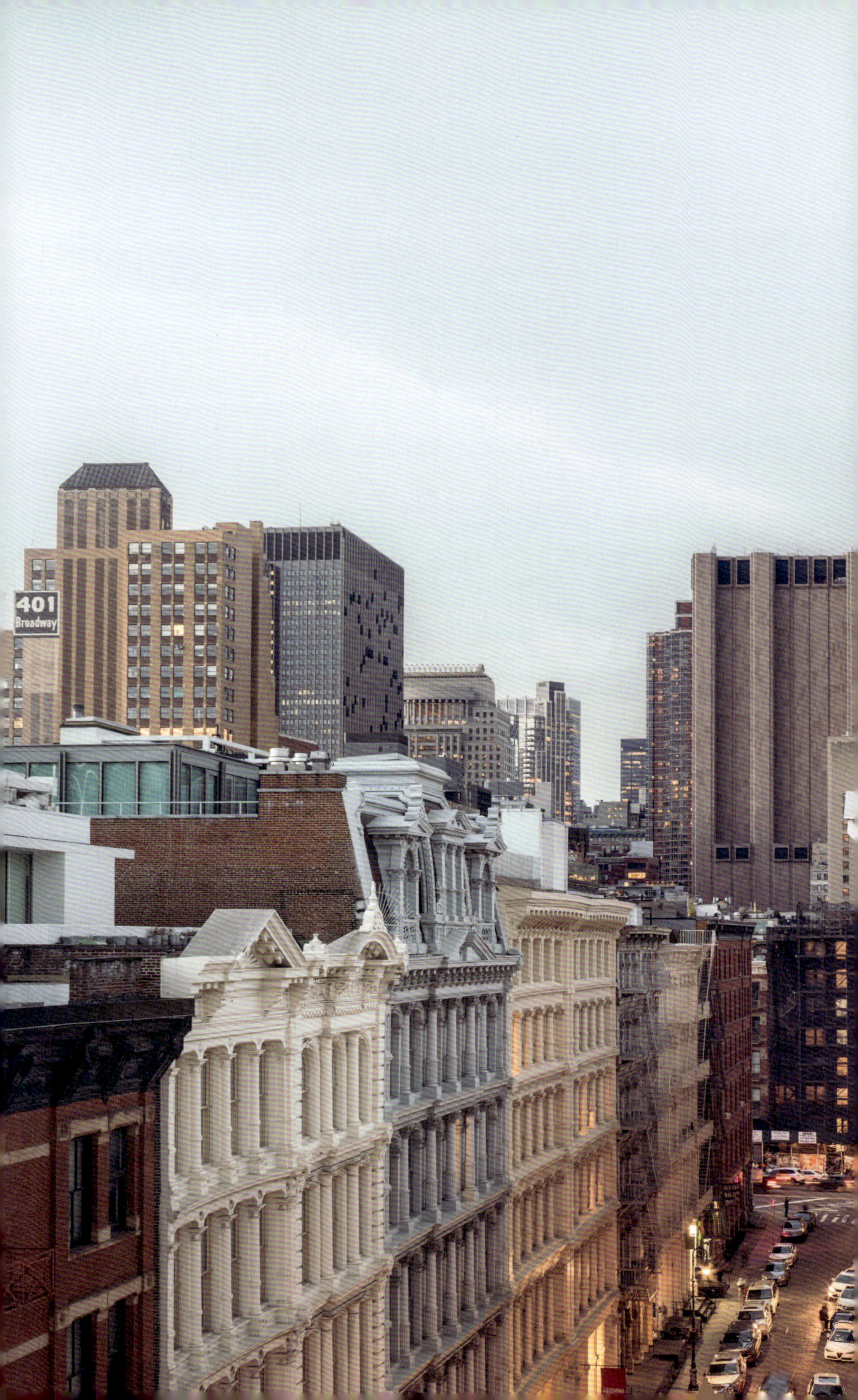
401
Broadway

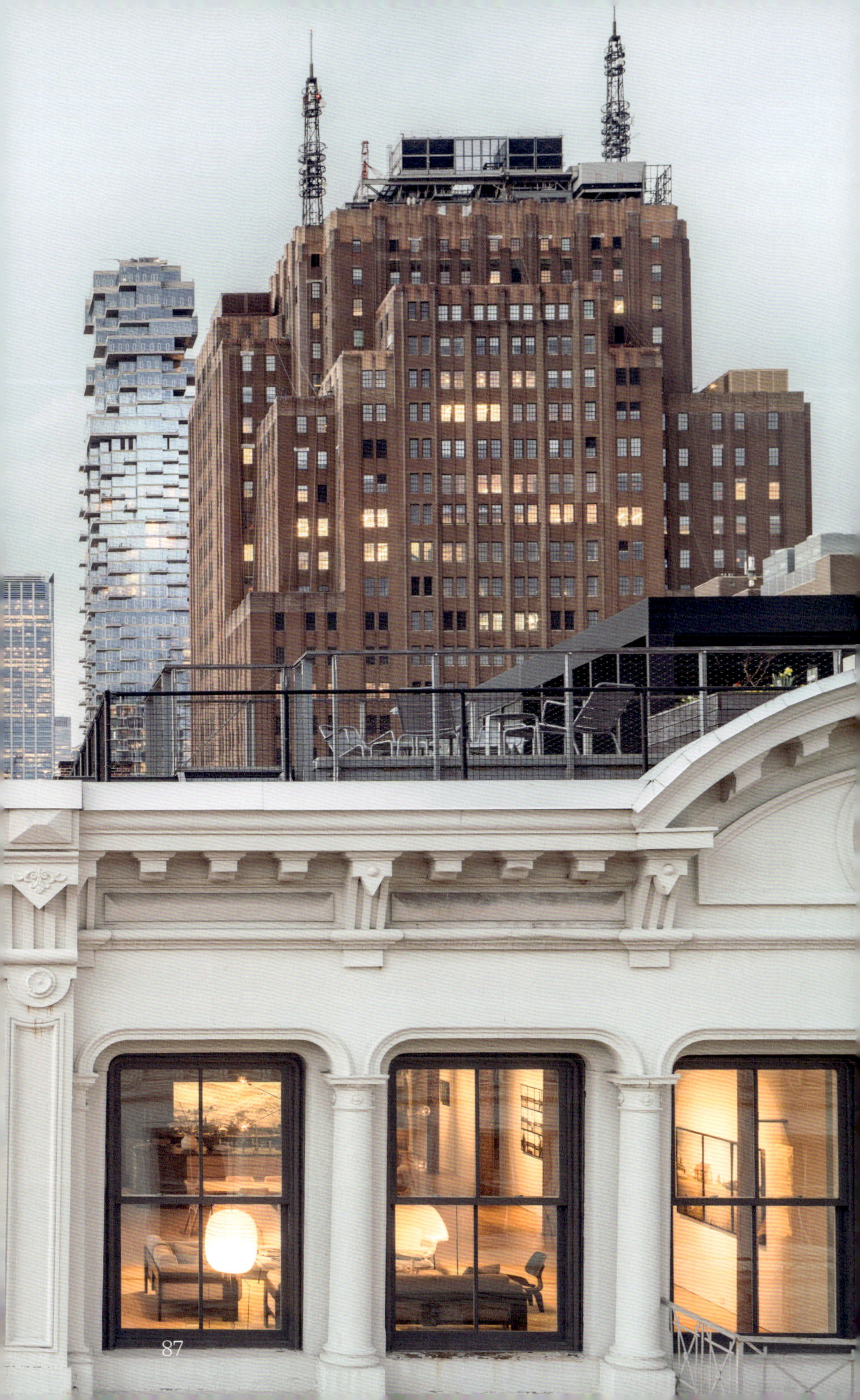

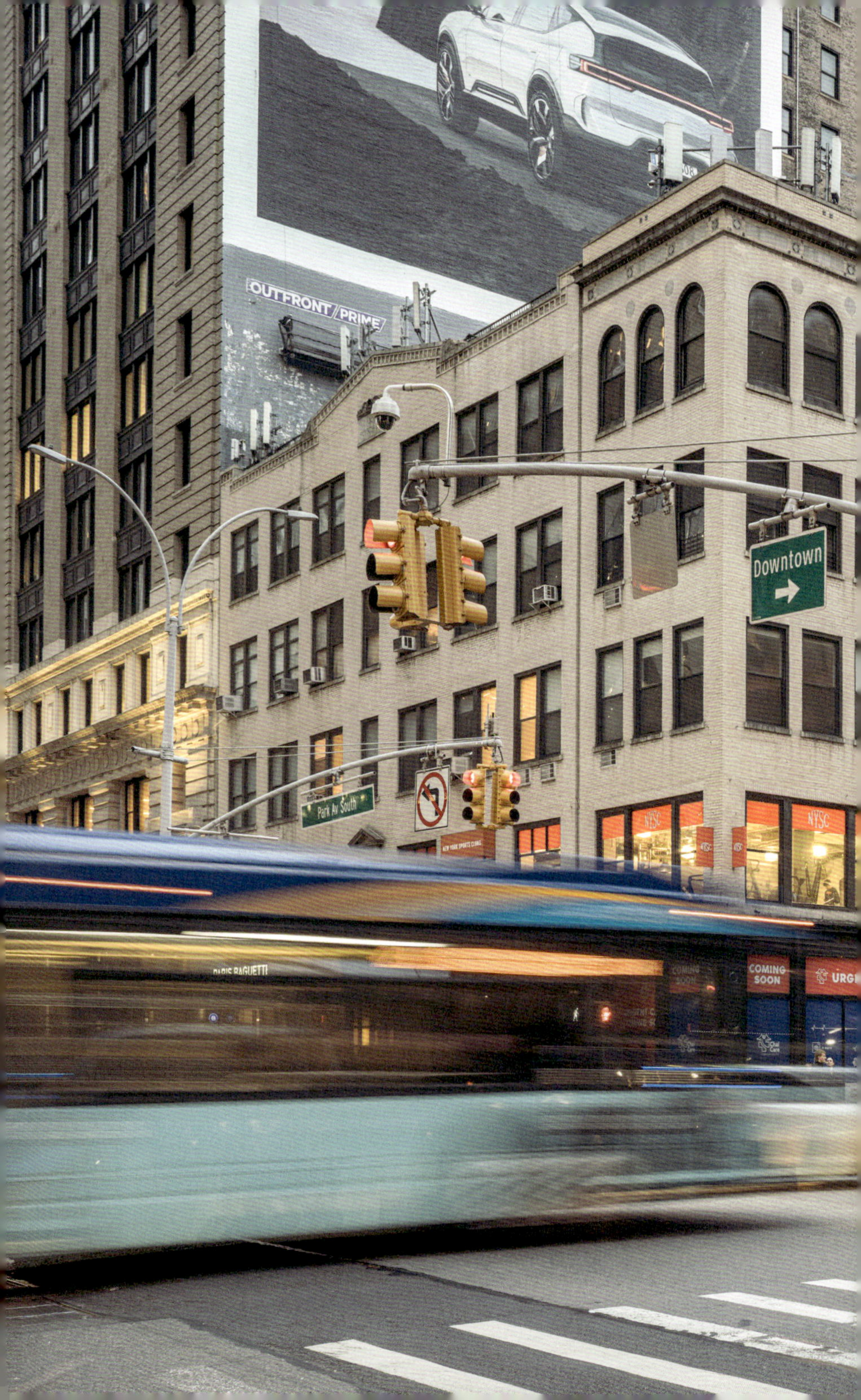
OUTFRONT/PRIME
Downtown
Park Av South
NYSC
NYSC
COMING SOON

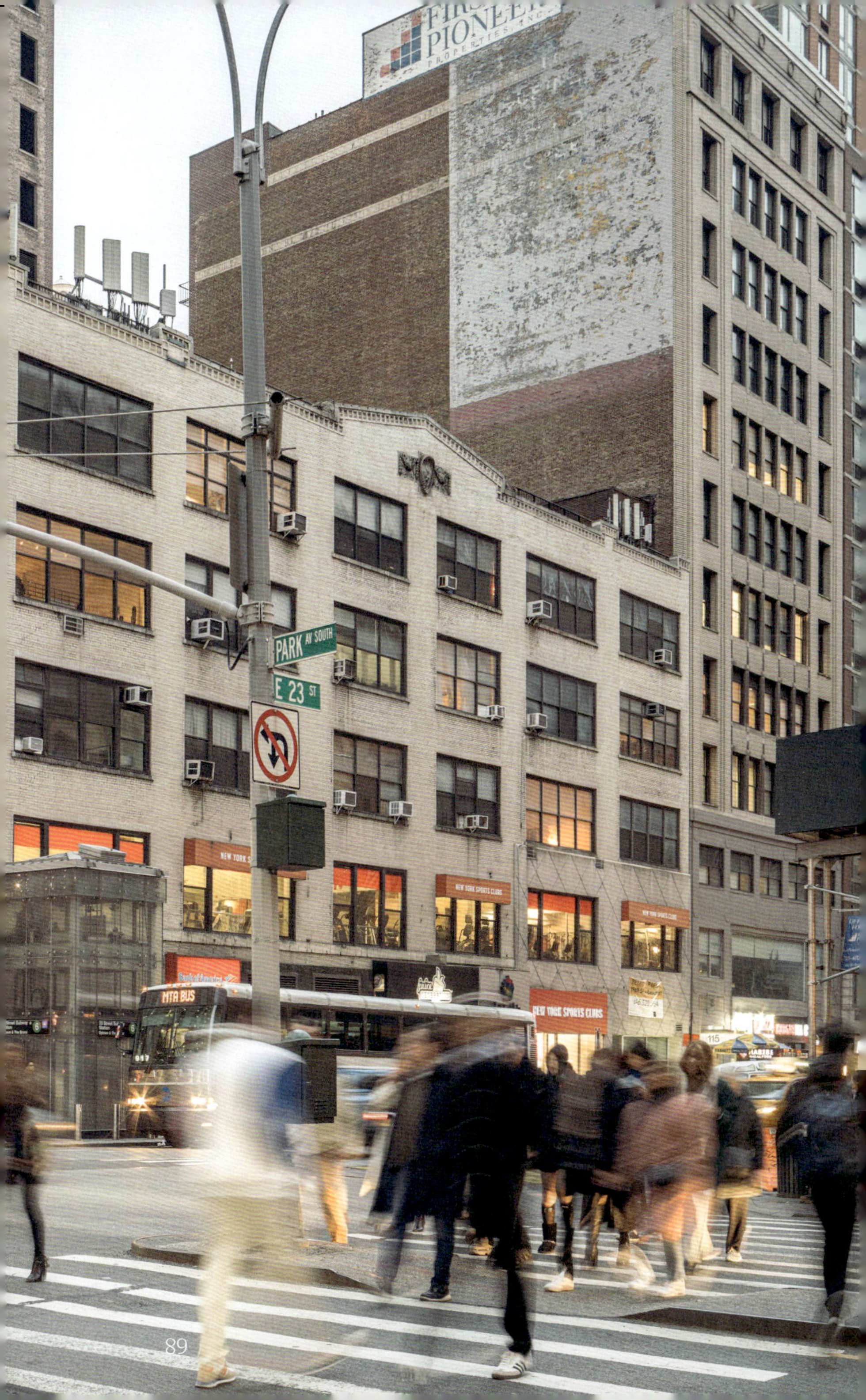
PARK AV SOUTH
E 23 ST
MTA BUS
NEW YORK SPORTS CLUBS

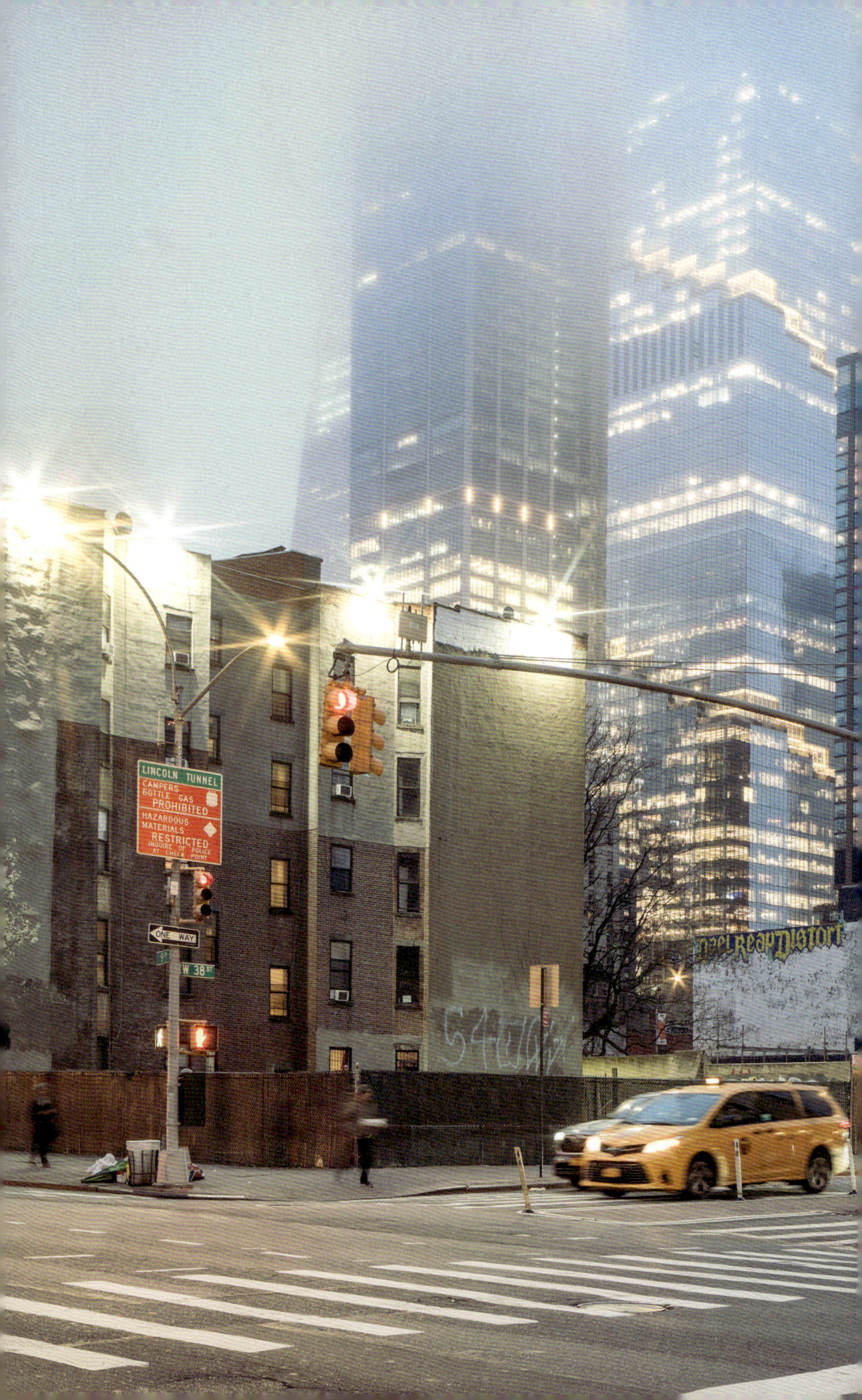
LINCOLN TUNNEL
CAMPERS
BOTTLE GAS
PROHIBITED
HAZARDOUS
MATERIALS
RESTRICTED
INQUIRE OF POLICE
AT CHECK POINT
ONE WAY
W 38 ST

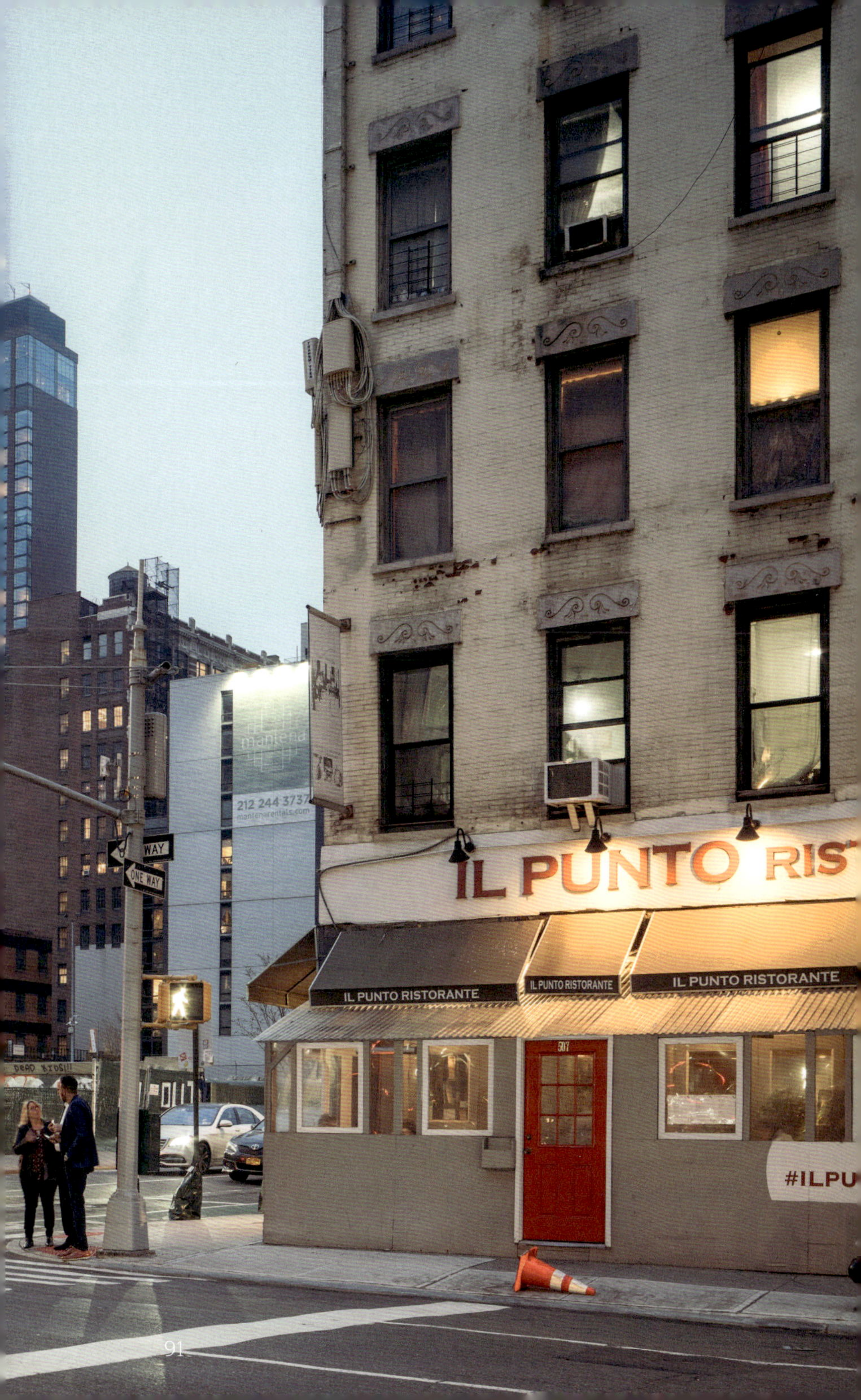
IL PUNTO RIS
IL PUNTO RISTORANTE
IL PUNTO RISTORANTE
IL PUNTO RISTORANTE
#ILPU
507
212 244 3737
ONE WAY
WAY

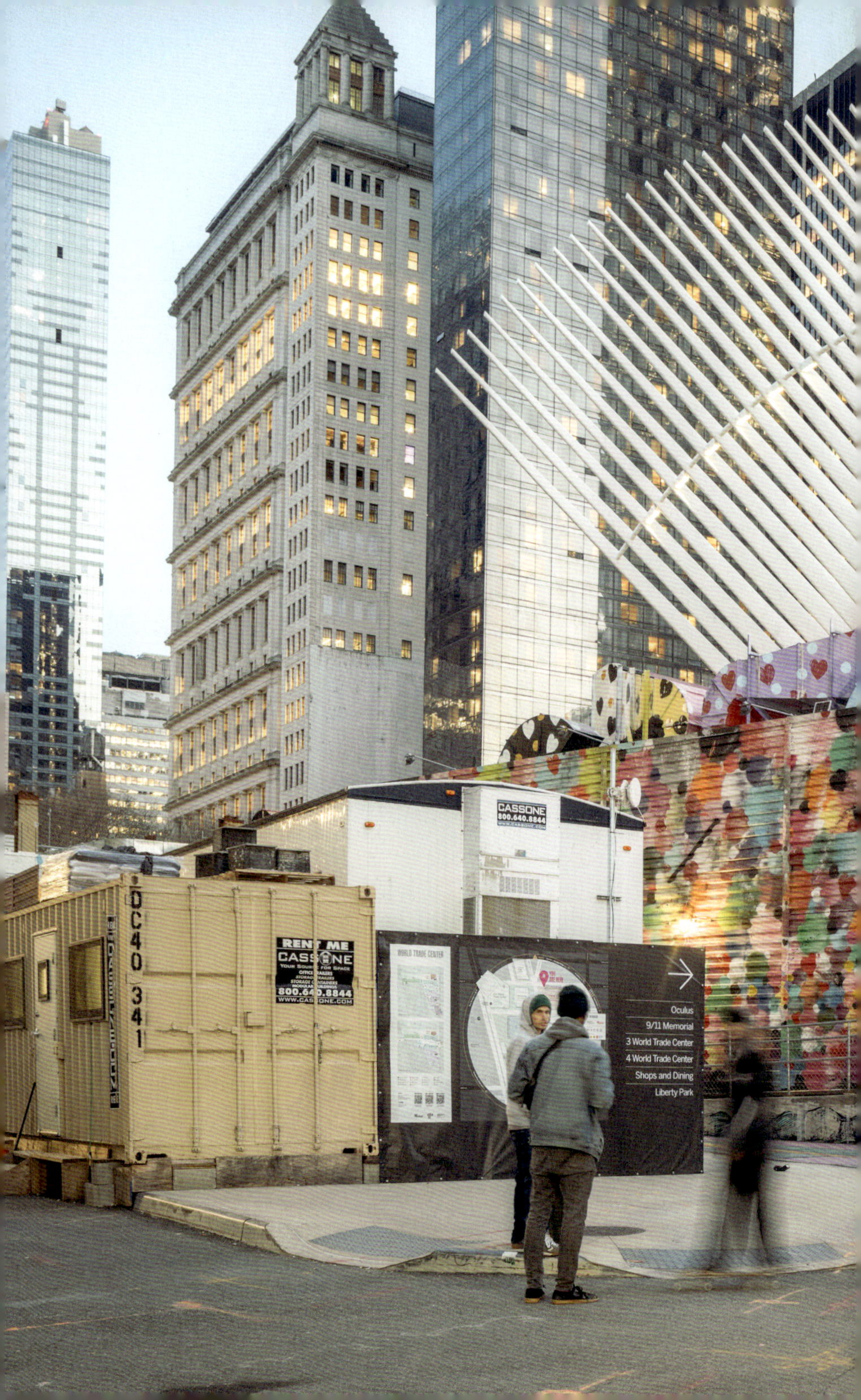
CASSONE
800.640.8844
WWW.CASSONE.COM
RENT ME
CASSONE
YOUR SOURCE FOR SPACE
800.640.8844
WWW.CASSONE.COM
WORLD TRADE CENTER
Oculus
9/11 Memorial
3 World Trade Center
4 World Trade Center
Shops and Dining
Liberty Park

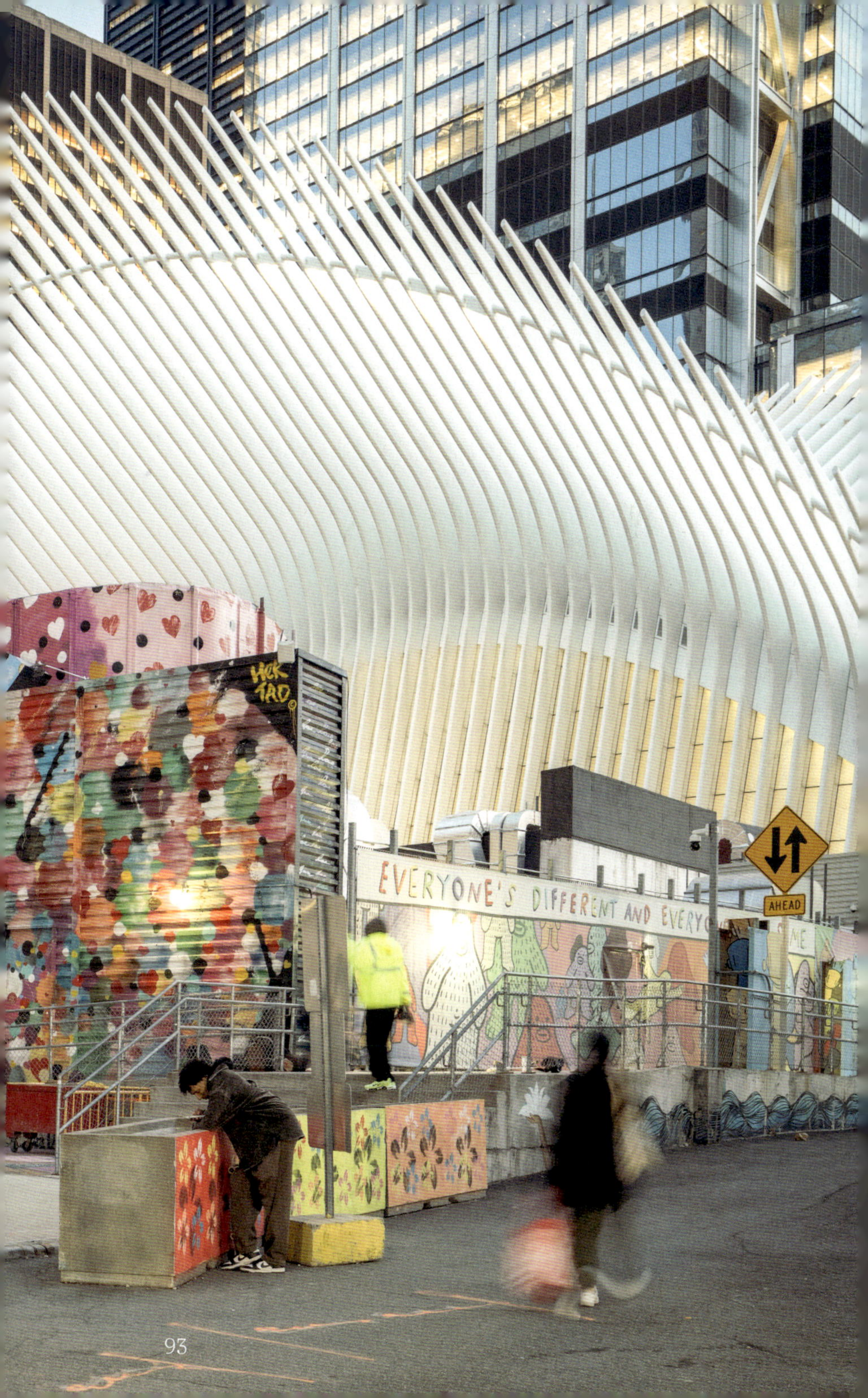
EVERYONE'S DIFFERENT AND
AHEAD

Previous Diaries

Cairo Diary #1
2014
ISBN 978-1-908889-20-1

Athens Diary #2
2015
ISBN 978-1-908889-29-4

Wolfsburg Diary #3
2016
ISBN 978-1-908889-34-8

Taipei Diary #4
2015
ISBN 978-1-908889-30-0

Kochi Diary #5
2018
ISBN 978-1-908889-44-7

Beirut Diary #6
2018
ISBN 978-1-908889-40-9

Wuhan Diary #7
2018
ISBN 978-1-908889-645

Zurich Diary #8
2019
ISBN 978-1-908889-65-2

Budapest Diary #9
2020
ISBN 978-1-908889-66-9

Osaka Diary #10
2020
ISBN 978-1-908889-56-0

Dhaka Diary #11
2021
ISBN 978-1-908889-86-7

Yangon Diary #12
2021
ISBN 978-1-908889-87-4

Minsk Diary #13
2021
ISBN 978-1-908889-88-1

Linz Diary #15
2021
ISBN 978-1-908889-90-4

The diaries listed above were published by *thevelvetcell.com* and are available on the website.

George Town Diary #16
2022
ISBN 978-3-96070-090-6

Unna Diary #17
2022
ISBN 978-3-96070-089-0

Sarajevo Diary #18
2022
ISBN 978-3-96070-088-3

Bangkok Diary #19
2022
ISBN 978-3-96070-087-6

Kuching Diary #20
2024
ISBN 978-3-96070-105-7

Turin Diary #21
2024
ISBN 978-3-96070-103-3

Wilson Diary #22
2024
ISBN 978-3-96070-106-4

London Diary #23
2024
ISBN 978-3-96070-104-0

New York Diary #24
2025
ISBN 978-3-96070-118-7

Vilnius Diary #25
2025
ISBN 978-3-96070-119-4

Istanbul Diary #26
2025
ISBN 978-3-96070-120-0

Norderney Diary #27
2025
ISBN 978-3-96070-121-7

The diaries listed above were published by *hartmann-books.com* and are available on the website.

New York Diary
Peter Bialobrzeski

Published by
Hartmann Books
Liststraße 28/1
70180 Stuttgart
info@hartmannprojects.com
hartmann-books.com

Photographs
Peter Bialobrzeski
bialobrzeski.net

Graphic Design and Typesetting
Sarah Fricke, Distaff Studio

Copyediting
Tas Skorupa, New York

Printing and Binding
Gutenberg Beuys, Hannover

Paper
Magno Volume

Typefaces
ABC Diatype, GT Alpina

First Edition, 2025
500 copies

ISBN
978-3-96070-118-7

For Tas

Thanks to the *Bronx Documentary Center* for the support